Cross+Walk outli... ...ans to enter into a new way of ... ... offers practical insight into Jesus' desire for us to set ourselves apart. The author concludes each chapter with thoughtful questions that challenge the reader to reflect on their personal walk with Christ. An absolute must-read for all born-again believers.

—Kimberely Payne
writer and author

Jesus asked His disciples to pick up their cross and follow Him. How is that journey going for you? Ron Mahler explores what discipleship means for us in our time. *Cross+Walk* is an invaluable guide for your personal journey.

—David Kitz
award-winning author of
Psalms 365: Develop a Life of Worship and Prayer

CROSS + WALK

Living Where the Kingdom of God
and Our Window of Time Collide

Ron Mahler

CROSS+WALK
Copyright © 2022 by Ron Mahler

Cover art by Janis Cox
Watercolour Artist

All rights reserved. Neither this publication nor any part of this publication may be reproduced or transmitted in any form or by any means, electronic or mechanical, including photocopying, recording or any information storage and retrieval system, without permission in writing from the author.

Unless otherwise indicated, all scripture taken from The Holy Bible, New International Version®, NIV® Copyright ©1973, 1978, 1984, 2011 by Biblica, Inc.® Used by permission. All rights reserved worldwide. Scripture marked CSB taken from the Christian Standard Bible. Copyright © 2017 by Holman Bible Publishers. Used by permission. Christian Standard Bible®, and CSB® are federally registered trademarks of Holman Bible Publishers, all rights reserved. Scripture marked ESV taken from The Holy Bible, English Standard Version® (ESV®), Copyright © 2001 by Crossway, a publishing ministry of Good News Publishers. Used by permission. All rights reserved. Scripture marked NLT taken from the Holy Bible, New Living Translation, Copyright ©1996, 2004, 2007 by Tyndale House Foundation. Used by permission of Tyndale House Publishers, Inc., Carol Stream, Illinois 60188. All rights reserved.

Printed in Canada

Print ISBN: 978-1-4866-2341-9
eBook ISBN: 978-1-4866-2342-6

Word Alive Press
119 De Baets Street, Winnipeg, MB R2J 3R9
www.wordalivepress.ca

Cataloguing in Publication may be obtained through Library and Archives Canada

*In memory of my mother, Mary (1930–2020)
& my sister, Linda (1958–2022)*

CONTENTS

	Acknowledgements	xi
	Introduction	xiii
	The Gospels and "Cross-Walking"	xvii
1.	A Different Kind of King *and* Kingdom	1
2.	God *Teaches* Satan	8
3.	Peculiar Love	13
4.	Avoiding the "Garden Path" of Pride	18
5.	Sufficient Grace	22
6.	The Waiting Room of Prayer	26
7.	Vine Dwellers!	31
8.	Are You Merciful?	35
9.	Promises! Promises!	40
10.	Sometimes He's in the Wind	44
11.	Blindness	48
12.	Forgive and… Reconcile?	53
13.	Jesus Changes Everything	58
14.	Ants… and the Faithfulness of God	62

15.	Costly Worship	66
16.	Soul Rest	70
17.	Rules… or Relationships?	76
18.	Losses and Gains	80
19.	A Word From *the* Word!	85
20.	The Ever-Relevant WWJD	89
21.	On Our Guard Against Greed	93
22.	*Being*… and Not Just *Doing*	97
23.	Peacemakers	101
24.	When in a Dungeon of Doubt…	106
25.	The Ambitious Life	111
26.	Water-Walking	115
27.	This Court Is Now in Session!	119
28.	Second Chances	123
29.	"Scoring" for Jesus	128
30.	Sign o' the Times	133
31.	Coming to the End of Ourselves	139
32.	Simon's "Cross"	143
33.	"Hymn" 22	147
34.	A Stone Rolled Away	151
	Afterword: Burning Hearts and the Emmaus Road	155

Stand at the crossroads and look; ask for the ancient paths, ask where the good way is, and walk in it…

—Jeremiah 6:16

Whoever wants to be my disciple must deny themselves and take up their cross daily and follow me.

—Luke 9:23

ACKNOWLEDGEMENTS

This book would not otherwise exist if it were not for the folks at Hope Stream Radio (in particular, Ron Hughes), who blessed me with an opportunity to produce a weekly program that I entitled *Disciple This*. The program focused on Jesus' interaction with the disciples and His teachings, which are as relevant and challenging today, in our "window of time," as they were to His initial, first-century audience. This book consists of a compilation of discipleship-oriented themes that were taken from texts of the above-mentioned program's various broadcasts, which I further developed to speak to the spiritual climate of our present day. Hope Stream Radio (a Christian internet radio station) is a ministry of FBH International that provides daily programming to English-speaking Christians around the world to encourage them in their relationship with Jesus Christ.

INTRODUCTION

Those we know as the twelve disciples shadowed Jesus on Kingdom-focused field trips that often took them into unexpected situations and turned them from mere followers into devoted disciples. This book, with an urgency that matches the social and spiritual climate of our day, examines what it meant to be a disciple of Jesus in the first century and applies those findings in our window of time. The prerequisites for entering into discipleship with Jesus are unalterable; they'll never change so as to "get with" a changing world. Anyone who claims to follow Jesus today must walk as He first called His followers to walk over two thousand years ago.

Those who aspired to become His disciple were given the terms and conditions. In the form of an inconvenient and rather disquieting caveat, Jesus issued one of His numerous shock-inducing statements, one that no potential follower wanted nor expected to hear:

> *Whoever wants to be my disciple must deny themselves and take up their cross daily and follow me.*
>
> —Luke 9:23

Jesus' disciples knew about crosses, and absolutely none of them would have drawn positive conclusions from this statement. For anyone living under the Roman Empire at the time of Christ, a cross left an indelible image of humiliation, suffering, and death on the psyche.

"Why does He have to use *that* word?" was likely the sentiment of choice making its rounds among those who had previously thought that declaring Jesus as their rabbi was a smart move. After all, the Lord had been saying and doing things with an authoritative chutzpah that skyrocketed far above anything they had heard or witnessed from any elder or rabbi, even the great Hillel (110 BC–10 AD). Jesus of Nazareth's unfurling ministry acted as a corrective lens through which writings such as the Mishnah, Talmud, and even the Torah were to be re-read. As Israel's leading teachers sought to usurp any influence Jesus had on the masses, the Son of God threw a spanner in their malfeasant work by repeatedly exposing their incompetence.

Putting one's hand-in-the-hand of the controversial God-man from Galilee and going along with Him was more than merely a voguish manoeuvre; it also meant taking an exhilarating deep-dive into spiritually uncharted waters. *Truth* was at stake, and reams of people believed that with Jesus they had struck the motherlode. The fact that the Lord irritated the religious police of Israel (the Pharisees) likely provided further impetus for some to get behind His growing movement, regardless of where its peculiar current swept them.

Students of any given rabbi (of which some were Pharisees) were to identify with their teacher, even to the extent of becoming *like* them. A *talmid* (disciple) would spend much time with a rabbi and even go as far as co-habitating with them. It wouldn't have been unreasonable, then, for Jesus to inform a potential *talmid* of how they were to associate and identify with *Him*.[1]

---

1   Ray Vander Laan, *Faith Lessons on the Early Church (Leader's Guide)* (Grand Rapids, MI: Zondervan, 2000), pp. 13–14.

Introduction

The Son of God came to go to the cross. Anyone professing allegiance to Him had to know that they may have to follow suit. While other teachers assisted their disciples in *finding* themselves, Jesus called His to "deny" themselves and even be willing to "lose" their lives in order to truly find them (in Him).

Far from simply being a hodgepodge of religious dos and don'ts that are designed to make us feel like we're good people or more loved and accepted by God, Christian discipleship is a call (as it was in Jesus' day) for His follower to enter into a radically new way of seeing, living, and experiencing life. It's an invitation to engage in a brand of discipleship that, at the very least, can sometimes seem like no fun, and at the very most, like boot-camp for stunt-persons and the obviously insane. It's little wonder why some disciples, after hearing all they wanted to hear from Jesus in terms of His hard teachings, chose to cut and run.

Becoming the Lord's disciple still requires a devotion to the Son of God that must be far greater than to anyone or anything else. Membership in His Kingdom has nothing to do with money, privilege, or status. The road in is neither wide, populated, nor popular. Being in the fold of God with Jesus as our Good Shepherd is to be in the pen of the ostracized and outlawed—of the down-and-out, the different, and the dissident. Despite the privilege of becoming a child of God who gets adopted into the family of God, cross-related costs also come with living under the roof of Jesus' Lordship.

Participating in His Kingdom requires that we identify not only with a selfless and sacrificial Saviour, but also with one who suffered to the point of death. The life of the cross-walking disciple of Jesus, then, consists of these three norms: service, sacrifice, and suffering. It's not the world's way of living, and neither will we ever prefer this way of life. Yet the godly walk, as costly as it can be, is still the greatest walk of all walks in this life.

Biblically speaking, our faith in and obedience to Jesus should lead inevitably to actions that reflect them. We can *talk* the cross all day; taking up our own and living it out (*walking* it) where the Kingdom of God and our window of time collide is an entirely different reality. For the Christian believer, every facet of life is mediated through their relationship with Christ, and the nature of that relationship is one between a cross-bearing, life-long learning "disciple" (*talmid*) and their loving Lord and Saviour.

You're invited to join me in walking in the seminal shoes and faith-filled footsteps of those who were the first to take up their crosses and follow Jesus of Nazareth. It is in those same shoes and footsteps the modern disciple of Christ dares to tread. As citizens and ambassadors of God's Kingdom, we do so amid a tsunami of spiritual challenges intersecting with our lives. This book endeavours to grapple with what that looks like through the lens of our increasingly unstable and darkening times.

THE GOSPELS AND "CROSS-WALKING"

Four particular books in the Bible were authored by four different individuals who were either privy to information about Jesus' ministry or witnessed it firsthand. These four documents collectively make up the Gospels of the New Testament. The didactic character of the Gospels helps the cross-walking disciple of Christ to observe what discipleship *is*, and then how to apply its peculiarities to their lives. In a world overridden by much *bad* news, the Gospels inform us of some much-needed *good* news. (The word "gospel" essentially means "good news.") In fact, the Gospels bring us the great and comforting news that God is still on the throne, and that Jesus still saves sinners and will return once again.

The biblical Gospels were written just decades after Jesus' death and Resurrection in response to forms of persecution that followers of Christ were facing. The Romans, in addition to factions of hostile, unbelieving Jews, held stakes in suppressing and even snuffing out the Christians' ecstatic efforts to evangelize the populace.

We would know much less about Jesus of Nazareth if these writings did not exist. Other extra-biblical accounts *do* exist, but only the four Gospels attributed to Matthew, Mark, Luke, and John were deemed reliable enough to be added to the canon of inspired

Scripture. In addition—and far more consequentially—without these four books we would have no practical blueprint from which we could observe and apply the principles of discipleship that the Lord laid down for us. We would be left without a clue as to how to be a cross-walking disciple; that is, how to know, follow, and live for Jesus Christ as citizens of His Kingdom, in the world.

If Jesus kept a journal documenting His ministry experiences, no one has been able to locate it (surely those pages would be *the* most coveted documents ever written). The Saviour didn't appear to record anything we know of in terms of His life and times. Yet praise God that we *do* have reliable writings, in the form of the four biblical Gospels, that preserve so many of the wonderful things our Lord said and did during His three short years of public ministry.

Some people wonder why there had to be *four* Gospels when some events are repeated by the authors in their respective writings. Others have wondered how accurate the Gospels are given that certain accounts are recorded somewhat differently between them. And why did some of the authors leave out certain things that others included?

For instance, the Gospel of John is characteristically different from the other three "synoptic" (similar in content) Gospels. John emphasizes Jesus' ministry in a manner altogether different from Matthew, Mark, and Luke. If you know anything about the original Greek Luke employed to write *his* Gospel, then you're aware that his writing style is very detailed and articulate when compared to the other writers. Perhaps being a physician had something to do with that. Then there's Mark, who wrote the shortest Gospel and who seemed not to stay on one account or topic for very long. His Gospel contains a lot of action. Mark often employed the word *"immediately"* as he transitioned from one account to the next. When it comes to Matthew, his Gospel contains more references to the Old Testament than any of the other three. It's also the longest Gospel, and provides us with the most detail in terms of what Jesus discussed in His Sermon on the Mount.

There's also a hypothetical source called "Q" that seems to have contained material pertaining to events in Jesus' ministry recounted in Matthew and Luke's gospels, but not Mark's or John's.[2] All this aside, the question remains: why was each Gospel writer so concerned with being different from the other three? Was there some sort of competition going on? Hardly! Simply, each writer possessed their own perspective of Jesus and sought to communicate that to their audience.

Matthew wanted his readers to realize that Jesus came to them as their long-anticipated messiah—the King of the Jews. Being very familiar with the Old Testament writings, he set out to demonstrate that truth. As a case in point, Matthew began his Gospel by outlining the family tree and lineage of Jesus. Mark, on the other hand was writing to a group of people who were associated more with the Roman Empire and, consequently, not as familiar with the religion of the Jews. Mark also wrote in such a way as to accentuate Jesus' *servant* qualities. This is also why Mark's gospel contains more accounts of miracles than the other three.

Luke wrote to a more intellectual (or educated) readership. As a historian, he was concerned that his accounts of Jesus' ministry were orderly and well-researched. It's likely that Luke didn't witness firsthand the accounts he wrote about, but rather sought to painstakingly pursue information from those who did. Luke's apparent aim was to focus on Jesus' *humanity*. Or, as is referred to in systematic theology, "Jesus from the ground up"! The Greeks were always on the lookout for the "perfect" man. Accordingly, Luke presented that Man to be *Jesus Christ*.

---

2   Charles B. Cousar, *An Introduction to the New Testament: Witness to God's New Work* (Louisville, KY: John Knox Press, 2006), p. 103.

Then there's John, who was an eyewitness privy to Jesus' ministry, often in the most intimate of settings. He referred to himself in his Gospel as *the disciple whom the Lord loved*. We get the strong impression that Jesus and John had a close relationship. This fact may have afforded John an inside track on how to communicate to his readers the wonder and significance of the infinite dwelling among the finite. John's purpose for writing his Gospel was to present Jesus as the *eternal Word of God* who became human "flesh." It's clear that John, in his Gospel as well as in the three New Testament letters he authored, desired to bring his readers to a deeper knowledge of and faith in Christ.

Suffice it to say that the Gospels we have in our Bibles are just the way the Holy Spirit willed them to be, as He moved each writer to convey their message in the manner they did. Each Gospel is equally true and accurate. Each is helpful, because the author purposely highlighted a different aspect of our Lord's person and ministry. Collectively, the Gospels provide Jesus' disciples with vats of observations and applications in terms of what it means to walk this life bearing the cross Jesus asked us to take up. Each author assists us in living where the Kingdom of God collides with our window of time.

The challenge for the Christian, then, is not that we lack enough information about the Lord. The challenge, rather, exists in our ability to remain obedient and pliable to the Holy Spirit as He aims to make our knowledge of Jesus more manifest in our everyday lives. We can call it discipleship, we can call it cross-bearing or cross-walking, but the call of Christ is—if nothing else—the task of living as members of His counter-cultural Kingdom, as He lives and reigns within us. And the four Gospels act as timeless and priceless guides on how to do just that!

CHAPTER ONE
A Different Kind of King *and* Kingdom

My kingdom is not of this world...
—John 18:36

In John 3, we read about a man named Nicodemus who approached Jesus in the dead of night. In the Lord's time, a disciple would often arrange to meet a rabbi in the evening after the busyness of their day was over. As a notable Pharisee and member of the Sanhedrin, Nicodemus likely wanted to remain incognito as he acted independently from his peers. As a distinguished teacher within Israel, Nicodemus came to Jesus with all his religious veneer and supposed theological acuity preceding him.

Likely an older man by the time he met with Jesus, Nicodemus's academic belt had much knowledge tucked under it. What could such a learned figure as Nicodemus want with Jesus? Was he looking to privately debate the Lord? Was he aiming to compare scholarly notes with Him? Why the out-of-sight, long after dark rendezvous with the one known as Jesus of Nazareth?

Despite his vaunted status within Israel, Nicodemus was clearly curious about the Lord, and perhaps even searching, spiritually, as he accepted that the ultra-distinct Nazarene he sought an audience with was obviously blessed of God.

After Nicodemus greeted Jesus and complimented Him on His heaven-sanctioned and no-less miraculous ministry, the Lord replied,

> *"Very truly I tell you, no one can see the kingdom of God unless they are born again." "How can someone be born when they are old?" Nicodemus asked. "Surely they cannot enter a second time into their mother's womb to be born!"*
>
> —John 3:3–4

Judging from Nicodemus's response, the term "born again" tickled his mental funnybone, even as it chafed against his Jewish common sense (see John 3:4–10).

To put the words of the quizzical Pharisee into modern lingo: *Born… what?? Did you just say "again"? You can't mean what I think you're saying! What you propose is impossible!* Nicodemus naturally thought Jesus meant being born again *physically*; our Lord, of course, was referring to being re-born from above (spiritually).

Jesus' interaction with Nicodemus illustrates that believing in Him is not as basic an investment as it seems.

Becoming "born again" and entering into discipleship with Jesus equals pledging allegiance to the Kingdom of God over all other earthly kingdoms, powers, and authorities. Even one's earthly responsibilities would have to take a backseat if Jesus was to take the wheel of one's life.

One individual in particular experienced firsthand what that kind of sacrifice looked like. A certain man who came to Jesus expressing his desire to follow the Lord wanted to wait until after his father had passed away. (It was Jewish custom for the eldest son to bury his father.) All the man wanted to do was fulfill his earthly duties as a son first before committing to enter into discipleship with the Lord.

While *we* might think it was a reasonable enough request to make, Jesus clearly didn't.

On the surface, the Lord's response to this potential disciple comes across as cold and lacking in sensitivity and consideration.

> *Let the dead bury their own dead… you go and proclaim the kingdom of God.*
>
> —Luke 9:60

Why did the Saviour, of all people, dismiss this man's request?

Jesus underplayed compassion in the interest of underscoring the kind of "sold out" commitment one must make towards Him to be His disciple and serve His Kingdom. A follower who is fit for service in Jesus' Kingdom is putting their *"hand to the plow,"* and taking it off and putting it on again is not an option (Luke 9:62). No waylaying of one's decision is allowed.

The kind of follower Jesus is looking to enlist must be willing to leave anything and everything in order to follow Him *now*. False starts only serve to spiritually skew the immediacy of the Saviour's call on one's life to be His disciple. There are no guarantees that one will get a second chance to commit to following Him (see Isaiah 55:6). This is why putting off a commitment to God until a supposedly more convenient time—no matter how noble the reason—never washed with the Lord. The Father was doing something revolutionary and urgent through His Son's ministry that still cuts against cultural norms and worldly wisdom—a perfect example being the Incarnation of Christ into our world.

Jesus could have come as a crushing military figure who'd slash and dash His way into preventing Calvary and the irreverent torture that went along with His eventual crucifixion. He could've bypassed all the ridicule and confrontations He encountered. He could've done without all the disrespect and blasphemous charges directed at Him. He could have removed the threat of the Romans in a heartbeat, on His way to reclaiming and re-establishing the nation of Israel at the same time.

Problem solved.

Yet Jesus is a *different* kind of King, who brought with Him a different kind of *Kingdom!*

I remember when I held my two children in my arms for the first time as newborns. Each looked so helpless and harmless, so needy and non-threatening. I wanted to do everything I could to comfort and protect them. A newborn child gives us the ultimate image of human fragility and vulnerability, and so it's difficult to fathom that that is exactly how *Jesus* came to us!

The Son of God arrived on earth as an infant who needed to be held safely within His mother Mary's arms. He breathed His first earthly breath as a King minus the pomp, in very humble circumstances—so much so that a feeding trough for animals was utilized as His crib. As far as we know, the only people who arrived on the scene shortly thereafter to welcome Him into the world, a band of nearby shepherds, stood on the bottom rung in terms of social significance.

Yet God would have it no other way!

In His freshly incarnated Son, God the Father was announcing, *He will not be your typical, earthly King. He will be a different kind of King and rule over a different kind of Kingdom!*

We don't have to get very far into any of the four Gospels before it becomes obvious just how different the Saviour was from any of His contemporaries.

In circumstances where others demonstrated anger, Jesus was calm. In situations where He was forgiving, others were accusatory. Where others perpetuated lies, the Saviour revealed truth. The Lord came to exhibit *heaven's* perspective on all matters and to fulfill His

Kingdom's agenda in spite of the whims and wants of the throngs hanging off of Him. Jesus wouldn't allow Himself to be pigeonholed by either fan or foe. He chose the hard road over an easier path to glorification. He chose to be around the sinful crowd while rebuking the religiously-acclaimed and self-righteous mob. He chose those who'd be the *last* to be picked for anything to be His *first* disciples.

Ultimately, He chose a thorn-twisted crown of mockery and an insidious mode of execution over a throne-worthy brand of popularity. As the ultimate friend of sinners, the Son of God did this for our eternal good.

It all works together to leave us with an innate magnetism towards the Person of Jesus Christ. Jesus made a difference when He walked our fallen soil because He was *different!* The eternal glory of His Kingdom's global manifestation is incomparable to all worldly kingdoms, which will one day pass away. When we enter into a saving relationship with Christ, we're brought into a lifestyle of discipleship that showcases the values of His Kingdom. This invariably puts Jesus' disciple at spiritual odds and on a collision course with a world held captive to the deceptive stewardship of the prince of darkness (Satan), a world which consequently operates in a perpetual state of rebellion and unbelief towards God and His redemptive purposes for it.

To be a follower of Jesus is to be part of a Kingdom that has both come and is yet still *to* come in all its fullness—a Kingdom that provides its blessed citizens with spiritual eyes to see the dichotomous extents to which the kingdoms of the earth differ from the one Jesus brought with Him.

In 1896, George Stratton, a professor at the University of California, was entertaining different theories in regard to how our brains process what our eyes see. To test his ideas, Stratton created a device to wear over his eyes that caused him to see everything upside-down. For eight straight days, while Stratton was awake he wore the contraption and forced himself to function in a newly upside-down world. Before going to sleep, he took off the goggles and blindfolded himself, the idea being that Stratton would be unable to see the world properly upright during the entire time of the experiment.

Just as Stratton had to learn to see the world in a totally new way, the call of Christ may seem completely upside-down compared to our normal perspective.

David Crump paraphrases the nature of doing life in Jesus' Kingdom by drawing a parallel between Christian discipleship and George Stratton's experiment:

> Anyone who wants to be my disciple must put their kingdom goggles on and live accordingly. Once you do this, much of what I tell you to do will seem upside-down, backwards, and inside-out.[3]

When we identify with His Kingdom, Jesus says we are to actually love our enemies and turn the other cheek when assaulted. We're to be willing to give over our only cloak to someone who needs it more than us. According to His Kingdom's values, if we have lust in our heart toward someone, it's as if we've committed sexual sin with them. If we're intensely angry towards someone, it's as if we harbour murderous intent. We could never have known the mind and heart of God—neither His intentions towards us nor what He requires of us—without the different *and* difference-making King of heaven in our midst!

It was the late Christian physician, counsellor, and writer, Paul Tournier, who remarked, "Jesus Christ is the dialogue re-established.

---

[3] Our Daily Bread Ministries, *God Reigns: Living Out the Kingdom of God, Chapter 2: Will We Take Jesus Seriously?*, available at https://discoveryseries.org/courses/god-reigns/lessons/will-we-take-jesus-seriously/.

He is God coming to us because we cannot go to Him."[4] The Saviour came to open the way for us to be reconciled to a holy God after our sin had estranged us from Him. Through His Son, the Father makes us children of God and adopts us into the family of God (1 John 3:1). That same Son is preparing an eternal home in His Kingdom for those who put their faith in Him as their Lord and Saviour—a *different* kind of Kingdom that now resides within a different kind of people. No matter who we are or what our situation in life is, Jesus is the kind of King we *should* all want to follow and serve.

> CROSS-WALKING: What attributes of Jesus separated Him from His contemporaries? Are you consistently exhibiting hallmarks of Jesus' heaven-come-down, counter-cultural Kingdom in your sphere of influence? Would people around you say that you are attractively different, as Jesus was to so many people who wanted to be around Him?

---

[4] William Barclay, *The Mind of Jesus* (New York, NY: Harper One, 1976), p. 23.

CHAPTER TWO
God *Teaches* Satan

Get behind me, Satan!

—Matthew 16:23

It's hard to fathom how God would have any business teaching His arch-enemy *anything*. God is light and life. The devil is about darkness and death. Where God reveals truth, the devil schemes to deceive. God is about salvation. The devil's bailiwick is temptation. What does heaven have to do with informing hell? Isn't the devil already a defeated enemy? What eternal use is there in making points to an immutable spiritual entity like Satan? Despite these realities, the Bible reveals that God proves various things to the enemy of our soul, and sometimes it's *His* people who get caught in the spiritual crosshairs!

How so? Enter one named *Job*.

Job, a righteous man like none other for his time, was oblivious to the epic battle taking place over his life in the spiritual realm.

The devil wagered with the Lord that if he had his evil way with Job, the righteous man from the land of Uz would fling his jaded halo for an opportunity to curse God. Satan must have been thoroughly gobsmacked to discover that after all Job suffered at the clandestine hands of hell itself, the humbled servant of God refused to throw in the towel!

Job was reduced to a human form of mush after he was hit by four crashing waves of tragic news. Each wave informed him of a series of events that resulted in the theft of his bevy of owned animals and the death of his shepherds, farmhands, and servants, as well as all his children. Mired within abject hardship and catastrophic levels of suffering, Job, instead of giving up, chose to *look* up by bowing down. During the absolute worst moment of his life, the only thing Job resolved to do was fall to the ground in a posture of praise and worship to the Lord (Job 1:20–21).

Then came the grotesque and painful boils Satan inflicted Job with from head to foot.

Job's wife despaired at looking upon the unrecognizable heap of misery her husband had become and counselled him to do himself in by cursing God. Job rebuked her with words that many believers today cite when they're languishing in the valley of darkness and despair: *"Shall we accept good from God, and not trouble?"* (Job 2:10). Hanging onto the thinnest threads of his faith, Job chose to give the goodness of God the benefit of the doubt. Job trusted that God is fair and that trials and tribulations are filtered through the same divine fingers as His blessings; moreover, God seemed to have given his stricken servant the confidence that even death is not the end for those who know the Lord and that one day his suffering would be vindicated.

> *I know that my redeemer lives, and that in the end he will stand on the earth. And after my skin has been destroyed, yet in my flesh I will see God.*
>
> —Job 19:25–26

No greater or more triumphant statement of faith has ever been uttered to defuse hopelessness in the face of suffering. Short of killing him, the devil unleashed all the free radicals in his wicked arsenal on Job, and the target of the evil one's campaign of pain *still* would not turn from his God!

This is not to say that Job wasn't confused over God's silence and seeming absence throughout most of his ordeal. It must have seemed to Job as if he was shouting his petitions into a tornado at times. Were his prayers being heard? Was he being seen from heaven at all? The lowest point in Job's suffering came when he wished he had never exited his mother's birth canal. The desperate queries Job mustered from within his broken heart, however, would reach a revelatory and restorative *breakthrough*. The glory of God would burst in on Job's pity-party and win the day, and in the end, Satan would be schooled (Job 38–42)!

Then there was Peter, whose faith the devil also targeted for destruction.

Jesus informed his most vocal disciple that Satan wanted to *"sift"* His followers like wheat (Luke 22:31). The devil desired nothing better than to take out as many of Jesus' disciples as possible, with Peter likely at the top of his hit-list. As it turned out, Peter's upstart faith in Jesus would be held to the refining fires for testing. A short while after Satan declared war on the followers of Christ, Peter would infamously deny even knowing his Master—*three* times.

It must have comforted Peter to know that Jesus had prayed that the disciple's faith would ultimately not fail. The Lord's prayer on behalf of Peter was obviously answered in the long haul, and—as we often say—*big time!* Despite his previous missteps and foot-in-mouth gaffes, Peter would become a tremendous source of encouragement and strength as an apostle in the fledgling years of the early church.

Taking Job's as well as Peter's brush with the covert operations of hell into consideration, it begs the question: what was Satan taught when he ultimately realized he could not get the better of these two servants?

The devil (in case his memory failed him) was reminded that both the *effect* and *extent* of his powers are limited by God, who can set the parameters and adjust the intensity of his evil work. Satan witnessed how his dark ploys play right into the sovereign hands and redemptive plans of Almighty God, whose will and purposes cannot be thwarted.

Just as the power of prayer can bind the schemes of the devil, so our claiming the promises and precepts in God's Word, in an hour of vulnerability, can make Satan turn on his heels and flee (James 4:7).

Jesus knew this full well. His employment of the Word of God when accosted by the devil in the desert nullified the evil one's counterfeit offerings. God, in the Person of Christ, schooled His archenemy in epic fashion over the span of forty days, prior to the commencement of His public ministry. The Word and Spirit of God, in powerful tandem, act as a weapon for God's people to combat the lies Satan lays as a snare for them. Although God is the supreme antonym of Satan, the opposite of God *isn't* Satan. The opposite of God is simply *nothing*. God spoke *everything* into existence. *He* is the ultimate reality. He has no rival. Satan, on the other hand, is not creative. The devil, in fact, is highly predictable and always up to the same old tricks. Satan is also defeatable (and has already been defeated at the Cross).

In these last days when spiritual ignorance, deception, and wickedness are increasing within every facet of society, the disciple of Christ can take solace in knowing that the battle not only belongs to the Lord, but has already been won by Him. Though it may seem like the powers of hell are gaining on God, the Bible declares the one who simply cannot and will not lose (God), and the one who cannot possibly win in the end (Satan). Within this war in the spiritual realm, God is always schooling and exposing His adversary (Ephesians 3:10, 6:10–11; Colossians 2:14–15). Though the enemy of our soul is real and dangerous, and none of us are exempt from possibly falling victim to his evil plans and pursuits, the devil is nothing to be terrified of if we're a child of God. Through Jesus Christ, God has already sealed His wicked adversary's fate, even as He continues to teach Satan why He is God and the devil is not.

CROSS-WALKING: Do you find yourself preoccupied with the powers Satan possesses, rather than those of a sovereign and Almighty God? What does the fact that Jesus defeated Satan mean to you in times of temptation? How might you be able to expose Satan's tricks and traps?

CHAPTER THREE
Peculiar Love

While we were still sinners, Christ died for us.

—Romans 5:8

In an untitled sonnet, William Shakespeare once characterized love as needing to be "rigid" while defining it as "crucial to endure life."[5] It was a rather profound spiritual statement to make, even if the English playwright didn't intend it as such! There are people we cross paths with every day who are starving for love—starving to *know* they're loved and to *feel* loved. We may not know their names or stories, but behind their faces exist hearts that are needful and crying out to be unconditionally loved: a kind of love that is constant, dependable, and puts no conditions on its object of affection and possession. There's an epidemic of people today who feel hopelessly lonely and who have never experienced a quality of love that fills their life with significance and security.

There are people all around us who continue to awaken each morning only to breathe in the air of a loveless world. Such people

---

[5] David James Niichel, "Shakespeare's Definition of Love," *Grade Saver* (https://www.gradesaver.com/shakespeares-sonnets/essays/shakespeares-definition-of-love), accessed April 3, 2022.

may feel like they have no love to call their own. Love is a many-splendoured topic: ask a five-year-old what they think love is and you'll hear a vastly different answer from that of a sixteen-year-old who has found their "first" love. Love means something *entirely* different to the couple celebrating their fiftieth wedding anniversary.

The Christian's knowledge and experience of God's love centres and grounds every facet of their life. Regardless of what goes on within them or around them to threaten their welfare, the child of God possesses a peculiar brand of love that brings it all into heavenly focus. Their knowledge of the unconditional and unchanging love of God informs their perspective on all things. It's a love that penetrates even the darkest corners of the globe in order to save souls and transform lives. It's a love offered to all and one, coming with a promise that's unmatched:

> *For God so loved the world that he gave his one and only Son, that whoever believes in him shall not perish but have eternal life.*
> —John 3:16

In my Bible I have substituted the word "world" in this verse with *my* name. This alters the application of the verse from a general thrust to a personal one. By putting my name where the word *world* is, I've taken ownership of the peculiar love God possesses for me in Jesus Christ. In other words, I have personalized this promise of God because I believe He is a *personal* God who knows me intimately. He has made Himself known to us in the Person of His Son. Jesus said, "*I and the Father are one*" (John 10:30). To know and accept the Son, then, is to know and experience the precious character of our heavenly Father's love for us (see 1 John 3:1).

This was one of Paul's burdens for the Christians in Ephesus. The apostle prayed that believers who lived in that idolatrous city would grasp the full scope of Christ's love for them. Paul described it as a love that is wide enough, long enough, high enough, and deep enough to forgive all our sins and lavish us with all the grace, peace, strength, and hope we could ever desire (see Ephesians 3:18). What a peculiar brand of love indeed! No human being, however loving, is capable of loving us as God does.

Some people begin to question God's love for them when mired in fiery trials and lengthy tribulations. In such situations even God's people can waver in their trust that He loves them unconditionally and is in complete control of the events adversely affecting their lives. The book of Romans, however, is clear that God's love can *never* be separated from us (8:39). It is impossible for the love of God to be marginalized by any spiritual or physical reality. No matter what adverse circumstance holds us, the unrelenting and ever-present love of God holds us closer. Sadly, our society is chock-full of people who are both estranged from and unfamiliar with this peculiar, one-of-a-kind standard of love.

The lyrics of late Beatle, John Lennon's song "Real Love" express this very reality to a T. While yearning to experience *real* love as a goal, the song concludes with the mournful resignation that the narrator is destined to be "alone." The lyrics are timeless in that they describe not only Lennon's generation but ours. There's an empty and hurting, love-starved world in need of being impacted and changed by the kind of peculiar love God's people possess and are blessed by. Although Jesus stated that the world will be able to spot His disciples by the kind of love they exhibit toward one another, He never meant for that love to be exclusively *confined* to the Church.

As a beautiful worship chorus reminds us, those of us who know God's love develop a powerful desire to "Pass It On."

To Jesus, authentic Christianity (or discipleship), can be summed up in one word: *love*, the quality of love *He embodied and demonstrated*. It is a sermon that is *shown*, not just spoken; one that is proven, not just pontificated.

According to the Saviour, the person who is most like Him is not the one who prays the most (the so-called "prayer warrior"). It's not the one who has a Ph.D. in theology, nor the one behind the pulpit of the biggest megachurch. Neither is it the Christian celebrity leader who sells a lot of books. To Jesus, the one who is *most* like Him and the most authentic follower is the one who *loves* the most. In His Sermon on the Mount, Jesus said His disciples must be willing to love even their enemies, and greet those who are outside their immediate circles of family and fellowship (see Matthew 5:46–47).

Clement of Rome (one of the earliest popes of the Church) described Christian love as being "without servility, as it is without arrogance"; a love that "knows of no boundaries, promotes no discord"; a love "purged of all earthly preferences for this man or that."[6] It's up to each Christian believer to embody and extend this peculiar brand of love to those outside the church's walls, indiscriminately.

The Saviour didn't play favourites. When He walked our earth, Jesus loved everyone. He loved the lowly and the loathed who were open to His words, as well as the proud and stubborn who remained closed to His ministry. He loved those who willingly took up their cross as much as He did those who shouted "crucify Him" and then put Him *on* the cross. The Son of God made no distinctions when it came to sinful humanity's common need of Him to forgive their sins. The cross settled all arguments when it comes to not only *if* God loves us, but also the unfathomable *extent* to which He does. We can call this peculiar shade of love, amazing and sacrificial—even call it "crazy" for that matter. But the peculiarity surrounding the kind of love God possesses for each one of us is ultimately grasped in how Jesus literally proved that He loves us to death.

---

6   Maxwell Stanifirth, *Early Christian Writings: The Apostolic Fathers* (Middlesex, U.K: Penguin Books,1968), p. 49.

CROSS-WALKING: Why do we find it challenging to love "difficult" people the way Jesus loves them? How often do you walk your doubts to the cross to remind them how much God loves you? When is the last time you exhibited the peculiar love of God to someone in desperate need of it?

CHAPTER FOUR
Avoiding the "Garden Path" of Pride

…rather, he made himself nothing…
—Philippians 2:7

There seems to be a rabid love-affair with "self" in twenty-first century society. Social media witnesses to the fact that we're more comfortable than ever broadcasting everything from our acquisitions and accomplishments to our attitudes, unbridled opinions, and even our "dirty laundry." Whether we're addicted to having to be seen and heard or prefer to live a more private and reserved life away from the public eye, it changes nothing of the fact that God has indeed created us for community, and for "others" to contextualize our uniqueness and affirm our significance.

This doesn't mean, however, that we are to attach prime importance to ourselves over and above our neighbour—and even more so, over our *Creator* (see Mark 12:29–31).

God has enabled us to respond to His self-revelation and to come to Him for spiritual life, sustenance, and guidance. It is He who defines our identity and worth and determines our place in the world. It is He who has a good plan and purpose for our life. Therefore, when we resolve that *we* are best able to create our own reality and foster self-satisfaction, it causes us to look away from God and shine the spotlight on us, as if we already have the Christian spiritual life figured out.

In the Garden of Eden, this is exactly how the devil advised Adam and Eve!

The cunning serpent essentially told Eve, "You got this!" (see Genesis 3:1–5).

By disregarding the clear command of God to not eat from the Tree of Knowledge, the first couple literally headed down a garden path from which there was no return. Deceived into thinking that they knew better than God what was best for their lives, they sought to help themselves to the kind of life *they* wanted to live.

This dirty deed resulted in humanity inheriting a fallen, sinful nature, characterized by spiritual brokenness and alienation from our Creator God. It certainly wasn't worth the mouthful of forbidden fruit that sealed the deal! Mr. and Mrs. Adam were not only the first humans to sin; it appears their taste for independence also laid the foundations for the establishment of the so-called "self-help" movement.

Today, the more independent you are as a person, the more you're applauded. Self-reliant, self-starter, and self-helping are ways to describe someone who's "made it."

In her incisive and biblically-based critique of the "self-help" craze, Stephanie Forbes links today's obsession with self-help to Satan's oldest lie (and sin: *pride*). In her book *Help Yourself*, she writes,

> Embedded in all the self-help messages I see around me is the tacit assumption that human beings can and should seek their own fulfillment on their own terms… this anti-Christian assumption has been making serious inroads into Christianity, and very few people appear to notice.[7]

---

7 Stephanie L. Forbes, *Help Yourself: Today's Obsession with Satan's Oldest Lie* (Wheaton, IL: Crossway Books, 2004), p. 63.

Forbes goes on to discuss 6 major lies related to the self-help movement that feature half-truths and all-out lies of the devil:

Lie #1: I belong to myself. Lie #2: I am entitled to a life of happiness and fulfillment. Lie #3: I was born for greatness. Lie #4: I can be as successful as I want to be, if only… Lie #5: I need to build my self-esteem. And Lie #6: I need to learn positive self-talk.[8]

On the one hand, the six "lies" Forbes presents possess an element of positivity; on the other, all of them are characteristically "self" oriented and even *prideful* sounding. If there's a glaring need in the end-time church, it's our need to hold to a biblically-sound theology—particularly a biblically-sound theology of the "human person" (*self*). Our relation to "self" will remain in spiritual check only to the degree in which we as disciples of Christ allow the Holy Spirit to fill us and transform our lives.

Some of the so-called "bigger sins" are derived from normal and even healthy desires within our heart that go off the spiritual rails. Sometimes what begins as a confidence booster can end up stuffing our ego to the point where we get an inflated view of our abilities and value. For example, when others praise us, we can feel validated and esteemed. Yet even seemingly benign accolades can be manipulated by the devil to ambush our flesh, resulting in all sorts of spiritually cancerous outcomes (see 1 Timothy 3:6).

In Christian teaching, pride is considered to be a capital vice, and one of the "seven deadly sins."[9] In the case of Adam and Eve, pride was the prelude to their eventual Fall (see Proverbs 16:18). Ungodly pride motivates us to see ourselves in an unrealistically favourable light. We begin to attribute good outcomes to *our* acumen and expertise, bad ones to the fault of others (see here Adam's pointing the finger at Eve). When others suffer misfortune, we can

---

8   Ibid.
9   "How to Ward off the 7 Deadly Sins with the 7 Lively Virtues," The Catholic Company (https://www.catholiccompany.com/content/7-deadly-sins, accessed 7/10/22).

blame them exclusively. Our problems in life don't usually stem from loving *ourselves* too little, but rather from loving God and others too little! (See Philippians 2:3–5.)

Choosing the way of selflessness, however, is choosing the way of Jesus. The apostle Paul alluded to this fact when he noted how Jesus *"made himself nothing"* (Philippians 2:7).

Selflessness is also the way of the cross.

Jesus could have claimed the spotlight for Himself, and would have been completely justified in doing so. In keeping with His status as God incarnate, He could have proclaimed, "It's all about me!" The Son of God could have been the most self-centred person to ever walk the face of the earth. Yet without denying His divinity, Jesus simply carried Himself like the sinless and irreproachable God-man He was and is. If we're to avoid the pitfalls of ungodly pride and steer clear of our culture's addiction to self and penchant for putting ourselves on constant parade, then we need to be willing to stand in the shade of Calvary's Cross.

The Cross of Christ, and Jesus' call for His disciple to take up their own and follow Him (to cross-walk), serve to deter us from pursuing the overcrowded garden pathway of pride. In making Himself "nothing," in order to accomplish our redemption, Jesus chose to empty Himself of every divine right, resource, and recognition that were His to take advantage of. The panacea for ungodly pride and our obsession with self, then, can only be found in the lowly and sacrificial ministry of Jesus Christ that culminated in His atoning death for sinners.

> CROSS-WALKING: How can seeing ourselves through the lens of Jesus' life and ministry help us to combat our tendencies to exhibit unhealthy/ungodly pride? What does it mean to you that Jesus "made Himself nothing"? Why do we find it unnatural to consider others more than ourselves?

CHAPTER FIVE
Sufficient Grace

My grace is sufficient for you... my power is made perfect in weakness.

—2 Corinthians 12:9

Are you content to operate in weakness? I can't say I know anyone who is. As finite humans, we are all too familiar with what it's like to lack the strength, energy, and desire to do something and do it well. Sometimes just having a conversation with someone can be overly taxing if you're in a weakened condition. Like many former pastors, I know what it was like to preach when I was sick or tired, sick *and* tired, as well as when I was sick and tired of *being* sick and tired! Preachers who preach on a regular basis will tell you that imparting God's Word requires much stamina, not to mention supernatural ability!

This is why Jesus' words to the apostle Paul should encourage every child of God.

But he said to me, "My grace is sufficient for you, for my power is made perfect in weakness."

—2 Corinthians 12:9

They're promises that were made by a Saviour who was tried and tested throughout His ministry. In the Gospels, the Lord established a habit of retreating to the hills of solitude to be alone with His Father in heaven. Jesus often required quiet places and safe spaces for rest and replenishment. Physical weakness characterized many a day for Jesus during His ministry years. On the cross, He experienced it in all its extremes, even to the point of unspeakable suffering. Despite this reality, our Lord overcame all that the world could throw at His divine resolve.

Perhaps this is why Jesus instructed Paul to content himself with operating in weakness. From what we read, the apostle was never promised healing, but rather, "sufficient grace" to endure his infirmity. Once a proud and overconfident Pharisee, Paul discovered that physical liabilities are nothing to downplay, for they summon the power-infused grace of God. Weakness and power are dichotomous terms that don't seem to belong in the same sentence, let alone the same vessel. Nonetheless, the sufficient grace of God turns human weakness inside out to reveal a far more wonderful spiritual reality!

Paul possessed a "thorn" (likely some physical ailment) that gave rise to God's sustaining power in the apostle's life and ministry. Outwardly, Paul may have appeared physically hampered and compromised; inwardly, however, the apostle was a grace-toting powerhouse! The book of Acts is a testament to the extent to which God overcame Paul's weakness in order to use His former adversary mightily in the spread of the gospel. This is encouraging, because we too possess "thorns" of various kinds and degrees in our lives. Their existence, however, doesn't exempt us from active Kingdom duty. Perhaps you have a "thorn" that is pressing in on you right now and you're wondering, "God, can you really use me like this?" Many of us have prayed prayers where we've cried out, "Lord, I feel too tired to do ministry today," or "Lord, I've been struggling spiritually and I'm so discouraged. How can I be of any service to you?"

But then God responds, "You've discounted my sufficient grace! In your weakness, I will be strong for you."

Friend, I have been there many, many times—not only as a pastor who had his fair share of personal and ministerial thorns, but as a Christian man and redeemed sinner as well. I am here to tell you that God *is* the thorn-buster! He *is* the sufficient grace-dispenser!

It's encouraging to know that whenever we serve God amid thorn-twisting seasons in life, that we're actually in great biblical company. Consider that some of the greatest servants in biblical history had a thorn or two to contend with. David, Moses, and Jeremiah, to name a few, served God under adverse personal circumstances. Each of them, at some interval, was cumbered by challenging physical conditions and/or environments, and yet all were granted God's ministering grace as a means to keep pressing on.

God is more than able to equip and empower His wearied servants. The grace of God compensates even for the weighty and debilitating realities surrounding mental illness in His people. God is as much the God of the mentally unwell and challenged as He is of the mentally fit and healthy. Neither the amount nor nature of the thorns we struggle with can render a sovereign God—who tags us for heavenly assignments—a non-factor. We can rejoice that He is a God who is Lord over *all* creation and, therefore, in total control of all circumstances affecting our welfare and ministries.

Whatever we perceive them to be, we can carry our thorns and challenges to the cross and lay them before our sympathizing Saviour, for it was there that, when He was at His most vulnerable and weakest point, He was also at His most *powerful*—securing salvation for sinners. Weakness is no respecter of persons. Regardless of our position in life, our common humanity makes us all prime candidates for experiencing the sufficient grace of God in our lives. Sometimes prolonged seasons of weakness alert us to this reality all the more. When the woman who was bleeding for twelve years touched the "edge" of Jesus' cloak, the Lord acknowledged that "power" had gone out from Him (Luke 8:43–46). In that instance, the woman was healed outright.

What an incredible testimony to the grace and power of God this woman would've possessed from that moment on! The power that went out from the Saviour *that* day is the same power that bids to indemnify any weakness or chronic condition besetting us today. No infirmity we possess is above or beyond the compensating and even miraculous reach of Almighty God. He may choose not to remove our thorn, but He will never refuse to add His grace to its effects. Like the apostle Paul, we too can rejoice in that those whose hope is in God *will* have their strength renewed (2 Corinthians 12:10; Isaiah 40:31). Although none of us wants to feel weakened and worn down, we needn't fret when we find ourselves afflicted by such conditions. What is *weak* in us is made *strong* in the Lord. God permits those who suffer weakness to be channels of His grace—sufficient, and yet powerful—and it's available to us at prayer's disposal.

> CROSS-WALKING: Do you find yourself sharing Paul's perspective of physical weakness? Do you trust God's grace to be sufficient in your times of weakness? How often do you reach for the edge of Jesus' cloak, as it were, when you're beset by weakness and infirmities?

CHAPTER SIX
The Waiting Room of Prayer

Jesus told his disciples… that they should always pray and not give up.

—Luke 18:1

As a precursor to his message, a pastor once posted a very provocative statement on the power point that read, "Prayer changes nothing." The potentially contentious statement reflected the season of life and ministry this leader was in at the time. Some among the congregation (of which I was a part) gasped as they read the line; it was as if their shepherd was committing the unpardonable sin! Others, however, resonated with the statement and immediately began to share their own frustrations with prayer—more to the point, with *unanswered* prayer.

In Luke 18, Jesus addressed this very issue with a parable—all while highlighting the need for *persistent* prayer in the life of His disciples. The parable spoke of a widow who constantly pleaded with an ungodly judge to grant her justice over her adversary. Jesus noted that even though the judge refused to fear God and couldn't have cared less about what people thought of him, he eventually gave the relentless woman what she wanted. Jesus said that His disciples are to emulate the persistence of the widow when waiting on God in prayer.

Over the course of their lives, many a disciple of Christ will find themselves in the "waiting room" of prayer numerous times. Perhaps you feel as though you're in that very room today! Unanswered prayer can advance our faith just as easily as answered prayer can. We can learn much about God and the mettle of our faith as we wait upon Him. Oftentimes, God answers us swiftly and according to *our* timeline. Of course, not all of our petitions are granted instantaneously. Breakthroughs in prayer can be a while coming. If the disciple of Christ is to endure, they must do so by exercising patience and trust as they wait on God to respond to their prayers.

Perhaps you're presently waiting on God to answer prayers for a loved one who is struggling in their marriage. You pray often but it seems like there's nary a change. Perhaps you've been praying for someone's salvation for quite a while but that person remains as hardened to the gospel as ever. Perhaps you're praying about a nagging health issue or for clarity when it comes to God's will about a certain situation. Perhaps it's a piece of property you want sold. Maybe you're dealing with a legal issue that continues to drag on and it's taking its toll on you.

Unanswered prayer can seem like a labyrinth that keeps us wandering within its maze of frustration, with no apparent way out. Instead of experiencing prayer as an intimate exchange meant to be enjoyed in God's presence, prolonged seasons of unanswered prayer can feel like a familiar dead end we keep coming to. Discouragement can set in, and after a while we may despair approaching the door to a room which asks us to come in and wait, and *keep* waiting.

What is the disciple of Jesus to do when all they get for their faithful efforts in prayer is the sound of heavenly silence?

It's been my experience that persisting in prayer should be the expectation rather than the exception. While we're waiting, however, we can be challenged in our belief that a righteous and loving God *will* come through for us. Sometimes we feel like we're through with praying about something and tired of dragging it to the throne of grace time and time again. How many of us have said, "I'm not praying about (fill in the blank) anymore!"—only to pick it back up and proceed to the throne of grace once again?!

The widow in Jesus' parable was seeking justice from an ungodly judge. We wonder how God could ever work through this magistrate who had no use for Him, yet Jesus said that this ungodly judge finally granted the widow justice after she came before him repeatedly. The point the Lord was making is this: If an ungodly person can do what is right, how much more will a righteous and holy God work for our good and give us what we need when we go before Him?

But here's the deal: it may take some time!

It's not that God is tied up with heavenly bureaucracy and our prayers have encountered some "red tape." It's not as if God has other priorities at the moment and our petitions have been put in queue with all the rest. No! God has a reason for everything He allows into our lives—even seasons of unanswered prayer, when He leaves us relegated to the waiting room of prayer.

Though we may not appreciate it at the time, God seems to favour testing and teaching His children *through* unanswered prayer and unchanged circumstances. The waiting room of prayer, in that regard, becomes the *birthing* room for growth in the Christian spiritual life. God often utilizes trials and tribulations as a tool from which to craft us more into the image of His Son. Seasons of unanswered prayer come straight from our heavenly Potter's loving hand. We're more interested in the product prayer can produce; God, on the other hand, seems to prioritize the process He puts us through as He brings about transformation in our lives.

Despite such intervals in the Christian spiritual life where God calls us to prayerfully wait on Him, He is just as excited to reveal His answers to our petitions as we are to receive them!

Yet the Lord longs to be gracious to you; therefore he will rise up to show you compassion. For the Lord is a God of justice. Blessed are all who wait for him!
—Isaiah 30:18

There's a peculiar sight that takes place at the Western (or Wailing) Wall in Jerusalem, where prayerful Jews and other believers can be seen moving backwards from the wall as they leave. The faithful do so out of respect and reverence for the presence of God, so as to not turn their backs on Him. Many devout Jews remain cognizant of the privilege it is to even approach Almighty God. Perhaps as we ponder more what it means for us to be in God's presence, we'll begin to perceive the waiting room of prayer much differently. The duration in which we're called to linger in our prayer closet is of far lesser significance when compared to the unfathomable privilege we possess to even address Holy God in that sacred place of prayer.

Every aspect of our lives is under His sovereign microscope. This means that God cares for every minute facet of our faith. Whatever concerns *us* concerns Him and His plan for us. In every circumstance of our lives, He is working for the collective good of those who love Him and have answered His call to follow His Son (see Romans 8:28).

Persistent prayers that go unanswered are a reality for every Christian at given points in their spiritual journey. It takes spiritual discernment to know which petitions to hold (keep praying about), and which to fold and leave with God. At all times, however, we must remember that we are praying to a good and all-wise God who holds our time in His hands, and who will bring about His best answer for us at *His* appointed time. The waiting room of prayer asks us to persist in God's presence, even if it appears as though His answer will never bust through the door.

> CROSS-WALKING: How might God be changing you as you prayerfully wait upon Him? What is Jesus telling us about the nature of prayer (as well as God) through the parable? How did you feel when God finally answered a prayer it seemed you had been praying interminably?

CHAPTER SEVEN
Vine Dwellers!

If you remain in me and I in you, you will bear much fruit...
—John 15:5

I'm often drawn to Jesus' teaching in John 15. In this chapter, we encounter one of the names for Christ in the New Testament: *The Vine*. The vineyard-like imagery Jesus employed in John 15 pictures sap flowing through a vine to its branches to enable them to yield fruit. This simple lesson in agriculture provides an analogy for how spiritual growth and productivity occur in the life of Jesus' disciple. God chooses to be alive within each of His children through their faith in His Son. As a result, those who are redeemed "in Christ" have His life flowing through and enabling them to live a fruitful, spiritual life (Romans 8:10; Galatians 2:20; 1 John 5:11).

Part of being a cross-walking disciple involves staying closely connected to Jesus (remaining in Him). This is key for His disciple to become the best version of follower they can be. For Jesus, every arena of life is an opportunity for His follower to *"bear fruit"* (John 15:16). Bearing fruit, Bruce Wilkinson says, involves allowing God to "nurture" in us "a new Christ-like quality."[10] When we're born again, we not only become a new creation, we also receive a new, God-oriented nature. Although a spiritual struggle rages on within us between our old and new person and nature, nonetheless, the Holy Spirit through the Vine of Christ helps to align us more with our new position in Christ.

The fact that God, who is perfect and infinite, chooses to reside within those who are imperfect and finite leaves us with some amazing spiritual realities to consider.

Although as redeemed sinners we're considered "saints" in the Bible, we presently remain in a spiritually fallen state and possess a propensity towards sin. To put that in theological terms, we are still unable *not* to sin. Yet because the life-giving Vine of Christ flows through us via the residing agency of the Holy Spirit, we can live a spiritually obedient and abundant life while experiencing God's peace and an intimacy with Him that is unlike any we can experience with any human being.

Many of us have at least one very close personal relationship, perhaps with a spouse or a life-long friend. Chances are, such people know us well and are privy to most, if not all, of the details of our life story—even the things we keep hidden from practically everyone else. We love these people and trust them with our lives. They have our hearts as well as our backs.

The Bible says that God, by virtue of His omniscience, knows us infinitely more than any human being ever could. He has full, unrestricted access to the deepest workings of our hearts and minds. There is nothing about us that we could ever keep hidden from Him (see Psalm 139:13–18; Jeremiah 1:5; Matthew 10:29–30; Romans 8:16–17). God has full knowledge of all our emotions. He has no need to be informed of what our cares or wants are. He knows more about us than

---

10 Bruce Wilkinson, *Secrets of the Vine: Breaking Through to Abundance* (Sisters, OR: Multnomah Publishers, 2001), p. 21.

we could ever know about ourselves, even if we lived to be two hundred! He is a personal God who waits throughout the day to commune with us. His intervention in our lives is always timed to perfection.

Whenever we go down spiritually unhealthy or destructive roads or get off our righteous track for a season, God in Christ prunes the non-fruit-bearing branches of our lives as an act of discipline (John 15:2; see also Hebrews 12:5–6). Conversely, when we obey Him and cooperate with His indwelling Spirit, He fills us and gives us everything we need to be spiritually productive and fruitful for Him in a fallen world. Oftentimes when we rely on our own strength and wisdom to affect a given situation, neglecting to ask Him for His blessing, we fall short of securing results that would have been more spiritually effective and God-glorifying.

If you're a pastor preaching weekly messages, do you lay your sermons out before God and ask Him for His power and blessing? If you're a student preparing for an exam, do you commit your studies to God and ask Him to help you retain your learning and recall it? If you plan on getting together with a spiritually seeking, non-believing person for coffee, will you cover this opportunity in prayer before you meet with them? In short, are you *remaining* in the Vine of Christ? As God's people, we have so many reasons to stay in close, prayerful contact with Him. Given the window of time we're living in, we as believers must guard ourselves from falling into spiritual complacency or becoming unhinged in the vibrancy of our faith. Just as branches cannot bear fruit if disconnected from their vine, so, without the aid of Jesus as the Vine, we are incapable of accomplishing any Christ-exalting good (John 15:5).

The power of God, for whatever purpose we require it, is there for the tapping through the Vine of Jesus Christ. It is He who has called us to a spiritually fruitful life; in fact, it's expected! Only a Vine-dwelling and Holy Spirit-filled life can equip and empower us to live holy lives that are pleasing to God. May we continually seek to cultivate this intimate connection we have with *The Vine*. May we, as His ministering branches, consistently bud and burst with fruitfulness. We were created for this. What a challenge! What a privilege! What a God!

> CROSS-WALKING: In what ways do you strive to stay connected and "remain" in the Vine of Christ? Have there ever been times when you felt acutely disconnected? How would you describe your life (spiritually) at those times?

CHAPTER EIGHT
Are You Merciful?

Blessed are the merciful, for they will be shown mercy.
                                                   —Matthew 5:7

In the Sermon on the Mount, Jesus lists the blessings that await those who live their lives a certain way. These blessings are known as the Beatitudes. They're sometimes referred to as the "Be happy attitudes," in that God will add His blessing as we strive to live according to them. As integral linchpins of spiritual truth that reflect the kinds of ethics and character Jesus wants His disciple to possess, the Beatitudes set the tone for Jesus' greater body of teaching in His Sermon on the Mount.

One Beatitude that continues to strike a convicting chord within my heart reads, *"Blessed are the merciful, for they will be shown mercy"* (Matthew 5:7).

We live in a time that is characteristically unmerciful. The world of the twenty-first century has morphed into an unconscionable free-for-all. A glaring neglect of humility, in tandem with callous opinions, has been maximized at the expense of mercy. In this increasingly godless age in our world's history, acts of mercy seem to be a long-lost virtue. Despite this growing reality of our day, we have the timeless words of Jesus compelling us to extend mercy to others that we may be *blessed* for doing so.

As we allow the Holy Spirit to cultivate a merciful nature within our hearts, we will experience a more contented and peaceful Christian life. We will be blessed because God, in turn, will be merciful to *us*. Our heavenly Father never overlooks our individual acts of mercy towards others—even the smallest ones—but rather "pays them forward" to us, to borrow a popular term (see Matthew 10:42).

At various times, we may have longed for God to be merciful to us after we messed up and let Him down. Many of us know what it's like to have had to drag ourselves to God's presence, where we cried out for forgiveness and longed for His mercy to dilute any consequences for sin. It is only because we do not fear being turned away that we can go to Him and find forgiveness and mercy as often as we have need (Hebrews 4:16). Thankfully, God doesn't harbour grudges and we'll never encounter a "sold out" sign posted at His throne when it comes to His supply of mercy!

It's one thing for us to desire mercy from God and others; it's quite another to offer it to those we're less inclined to extend it to. In our longing to be made right with God after *we've* sinned, we must also remember that there may be people who've wronged us and long for us to be merciful to them.

So let me ask you: Are *you* a merciful person? Does it depend on the person or the situation? Are you more favourable towards some and not others? In a section of Paul's letter to the believers in Rome, the apostle wrote about spiritual gifts (as he also did in 1 Corinthians 12). However, in his counsel to the church in Rome, Paul lists "mercy" as being one of the spiritual gifts that some Christians are endowed with (Romans 12:8). Though every disciple of Christ is called to be merciful in character, God has wired certain believers with the spiritual propensity to exhibit mercy in gifted fashion.

Whether or not we possess the gift of mercy, we are most like our Saviour when we are merciful towards others. In our endless process of being conformed to the likeness of Christ, bestowing acts of *mercy* is integral.

The Bible, in fact, is a veritable apology for the merciful nature of God.

Throughout both the Old and New Testaments, we can find witnesses to the depths of God's mercy. Psalm 103:10 says that God *"does not treat us as our sins deserve or repay us according to our iniquities."* In Ephesians, Paul wrote that the God who saved us is *"rich in mercy"* (2:4). God, then, desires for His children to be merciful towards people who *don't* deserve it, just as He is. Mercy, however, can never be a "right" any offender can claim. It is granted freely and based on the intentions of the giver to the recipient. Mercy, in its essence, is choosing *not* to treat another person according to how they've offended us. It is the anti eye-for-an-eye. The child of God acts mercifully as a selfless concession they willingly make, not begrudgingly.

The merciful disciple considers lightening the consequences of another person's sin against them. At the same time, extending mercy does not mean refusing to confront or hold someone accountable for their actions and sin. We do someone little spiritual good if we choose to overlook whatever they did that has grieved God and/or has violated us and our trust in them. Yet even a seemingly insignificant act of mercy can become a powerful change-agent in the life of a person we extend it to. Mercy, if nothing else, is *ministry!*

Jesus wants those of us who are recipients of His rich mercy to be generous reflectors and dispensers of it, not spiritually myopic and ungrateful hoarders of it. There will always be people who come and go in our life who will challenge our willingness and ability to be merciful. In our so-called "cancel culture," where we treat people as objects of scorn and heartlessly shove them out of social and professional circles, mercy remains a breath of heavenly fresh air in a suffocating world of gracelessness.

In the Beatitude, Jesus is saying that wherever God's people factor in, mercy must be accounted for as well. Mercy redirects both the offender and the offended back towards Calvary, where the One suffering in our place—Jesus Christ—decided to have mercy on all.

God didn't owe us mercy. Neither did He owe us a pardon. *We* put ourselves on the hook of His judgment. *We* sinned against *Him*. Despite our transgression, our Father in heaven lovingly chose to cover our sin with the precious blood of His Son. What a life—what a world-transforming reality we embody as Christians!

Amid the billions inhabiting the earth, God's people should be head and shoulders above the crowd in their ability to be merciful. Acts of mercy between believers aid the Church's witness and help its message to grow fruitful legs. For that reason, mercy must begin with God's house and be modelled by His people for the world to behold. Accordingly, Paul exhorted the early believers to bear with one another and forgive each other as Christ forgave them (Colossians 3:13). As a once-hater and persecutor of Christians, the apostle admitted to being a benefactor of God's great mercy himself (1 Timothy 1:16). James noted that *"Mercy triumphs over judgment"* in that an act of mercy promotes reconciliation between people, and fosters closeness between the merciful person and God (2:13). Jude implored the Christians under his care to be merciful toward fellow believers whose faith was weak and wavering (22). All of God's people are, in fact, to *love* mercy (Micah 6:8). The Bride of Christ was created to be a shining city on a hill whose righteous rays enlighten the world's indifference to its presence. Our capacity as God's people to exhibit mercy plays an integral role in accomplishing just that.

CROSS-WALKING: Can you recall a time when someone extended mercy to you? Why is mercy different from simply overlooking someone's offense against us? Can you recall the last time you extended mercy to someone who sinned against you?

CHAPTER NINE
Promises! Promises!

All you need to say is simply "Yes" or "No"...
—Matthew 5:37

At some point in our lives, most—if not all—of us have made a promise we couldn't keep. We likely intended to keep our word, but for whatever reason, we failed to. In life, it's always better to be known as a promise-*keeper* than as merely a promise-*maker*. Who wouldn't want to be known as a person who keeps the promises they make to others? When a man and woman get married, that is essentially what they do before God and gathered witnesses. They may be called marriage "vows," but for all intents and purposes, they're *promises* we're holding ourselves to for the benefit of someone else.

When broken or unfulfilled promises begin to litter the resume of our character, consequences abound. Many a reputation has been marred on account of people whom others deem too unreliable to be trusted. Others may become less inclined to confide in such people or depend on them for help.

We're living in a day where we have largely lost faith in people's word, especially those that come in the form of promises made by politicians and governments. We live in a time where we've become conditioned to expect that a lot of the promises people make will *not* be kept. There are individuals all around us whose lives showcase what broken promises look like. I once encountered an individual who told me how his whole life, including his marriage of forty years, fell apart because he refused to keep his promise to get help for substance abuse. When it comes to broken promises, the degree of consequences can vary.

Perhaps the most consequential of all broken promises are the ones we made to God and failed to keep.

Peter could attest to that. The disciple's infamous promise to not abandon Jesus, and subsequent breaking of that promise, could've defined and ultimately derailed his life.

We're familiar with the scene. After Jesus and His disciples had their last meal together during the Passover (shortly before He was crucified), the Lord informed the Twelve that all of them would soon fall away and desert Him. The disciples must have known in their heart of hearts that what Jesus prophesied *was* possible. Although they likely felt that they *should* and *would* stick with their Master come what may, the Son of God knew what they couldn't have.

Then, Peter, while trying a little bravado on for size, steps up to the plate and takes a swing at a hasty promise. The disciple pledged to stay by the Lord's side all the way, even if that loyalty led to uncharted or dangerous destinations. Peter's well-intentioned promise inspired his fellow disciples to follow in domino fashion. One by one, they all agreed to never abandon their Lord. Their collective, risk-soaked pledge—riding on the coat-tails of Peter's initial resolve to never desert their Master—was premature at best.

Taking oaths and making vows was nothing new to the Jewish people. Such practices were woven into the social fabric of Israel's cultural and religious customs. Oaths, however, were often accompanied by pronounced curses as a consequence in the event that the oath-taker failed to follow through with the promise they made before the Lord (see Numbers 5:19–22; Nehemiah 5:12–13; 2 Samuel 3:9). This may explain why Peter called curses down on himself after he ended up doing what he vowed he *wouldn't* do: abandoning Jesus and denying even knowing Him. Even the evil Jezebel, a Gentile from Phoenicia, vowed to kill the prophet Elijah or face the wrath of the gods (1 Kings 19:2).

Disciples of Jesus, then, must carefully weigh what they're promising others. Before we make a promise, we should consider the following questions: Are we being entirely honest about our intent or are we just trying to impress? Is the promise we're making realistic? What are possible obstacles that might prevent us from keeping our promise? If the promise goes unfulfilled, what consequences could that pose for others and even ourselves? Whether the world takes its oaths and vows seriously or not, God takes the ones His people make quite seriously.

Consider Jesus' words in Matthew's gospel:

Again, you have heard that it was said to the people long ago, "Do not break your oath, but fulfill to the Lord the vows you have made." But I tell you, do not swear an oath at all: either by heaven, for it is God's throne; or by the earth, for it is his footstool; or by Jerusalem, for it is the city of the Great King. And do not swear by your head, for you cannot make even one hair white or black. All you need to say is simply "Yes" or "No"; anything beyond this comes from the evil one.
—Matthew 5:33–37

If we claim to be people of *the* Word, then we must be known as people of *our* word. The perceptive Greek playwright and thinker Aeschylus (525–456 BC) said, "It is not the oath that makes us believe the [person], but the person of the oath."[11] God's people are

---

11 https://www.goodreads.com/author/quotes/990.Aeschylus

to be known for being promise *keepers*, not wafflers. Jesus desires that His disciples set themselves apart from the fickle kinds of promises and commitments made by many in our fallen world. The disciple of Christ is to strive to be a man or a woman of honesty and integrity—which are not only priceless jewels in the crown of Christian character, but sorely lacking in society as a whole today.

> CROSS-WALKING: Do you typically find it hard to keep promises? Why was Jesus so concerned about His disciples being people of their word? What might unfulfilled promises have to do with the devil?

CHAPTER TEN
Sometimes He's in the Wind

He makes winds his messengers...
　　　　　　　　　　　　　　—Psalm 104:3–4

Wind imagery, in Scripture, is used to symbolize the unseen presence and purpose of God. In the book of Genesis, the Lord caused the wind to pass over the earth, resulting in the flood waters subsiding (8:1). It was a strong easterly wind the Lord manipulated that made a pathway within the heart of the Red Sea for the Israelites to safely walk through (Exodus 14:21). In Psalm 1:4–5, the wicked person's inability to *"stand in the judgment"* is envisaged as a blustery turn of events. The *"wicked"* are like *"chaff"* that the wind blows away, says the psalmist. In the book of Job, the Lord speaks to His grief-stricken servant out of a whirlwind (Job 38:1). Even the anger and vengeance of God is captured in terms such as *"storm"* by the prophet Nahum (1:3).

The Gospels depict Jesus as being at the sovereign helm of creation, able to calm the wind and waves at His command. In Matthew 24, the Lord prophesies that God will gather up the faithful who died during the Great Tribulation from the four winds (24:31). As we survey the Bible, we find that *all* creation exists to serve God's redemptive purposes and plans (Psalm 104:3–4). Jesus likened the movement of the Holy Spirit to the wind's effect: we can "hear" it around us but cannot detect where it comes from or where it's headed. The Saviour was drawing a parallel from the physical to the spiritual. Interestingly, the words "Spirit" and "wind" in John 3:8 are derived from the same Greek word, *pneuma*.[12]

Just as we can see how the wind flaps the branches and leaves of trees but are unable to actually *see* the wind in physical form, so the Holy Spirit—though we cannot physically see when He enters an individual—provides proof of His effectual residence *within* that person. Eventually we begin to see a spiritual transformation take place in the life of someone who is born again (John 3:3). Such a person begins to exhibit forms of spiritual fruit that the Holy Spirit produces inwardly (see Galatians 5:22–23). Consequently, the person God created us—and indeed *saved* us—to be becomes increasingly visible outwardly as He fashions the new believer into the likeness of Christ.

Of course, this doesn't mean that our redeemed lives will be exempt from spiritual challenges and battles. We could never expect God to allow only favourable gusts to blow upon our lives. We shouldn't be surprised, then, when spiritually stormy fronts move in on us, bringing their share of inward and outward calamity, tension, and struggle.

We can resist the Spirit's cleansing work in our lives. We can grieve Him and quench His refining fire that aims to burn away old, sinful patterns of behaviour and replace them with new, God-pleasing ones. We can rebel and enter into seasons of disobedience. Though our faith may teeter a little here and totter some more there, our redemption is grounded in the fact that Christ died for us and His Spirit yet indwells us—His temple. Thankfully, those who are born again can never fall so far as to *lose* their salvation. At the moment in

---

12 James Strong, *Strong's Comprehensive Concordance of the Bible* (Grand Rapids, MI: World Publishing), p. 58.

which we put our faith in Jesus as our Saviour, we are sealed by the Spirit and simultaneously granted eternal security in our salvation (Ephesians 1:13).

This is what the Bible teaches about spiritual regeneration. When we put our believing faith in Jesus Christ, the Holy Spirit enters our lives and redeems us from death and eternal separation from God. Throughout our spiritual pilgrimage, the Spirit remains active and missional within us and around us, blowing at will. However, we can't always know right away what the Holy Spirit is up to in relation to the specific will of God, nor discern which direction He wills to point us in as He guides us.

Before the bewildered eyes of Elisha, the Lord swept the prophet Elijah up to heaven in a whirlwind, never to be seen again (2 Kings 2:11). Fresh from His baptism, Jesus followed the Spirit into the desert for forty days of pre-ministry testing and preparation (Luke 4:1). Immediately after Philip baptized the Ethiopian eunuch, the Holy Spirit suddenly took the apostle away, only for him to appear in another location (see Acts 8:39). When the wind of God, in the Person of the Spirit, is blowing, we need not fear its providence. His grace flows through every cross-breeze He sends along the pathways of our spiritual pilgrimage. Therefore, we can head into His wind in sheer delight, knowing it blows on purpose!

The next time we look around and observe the wind's effect within nature, may we be reminded of how God is *super*naturally as well as sovereignly at work within and around us. We never know where He's headed or where He's working until we see His ministry's handiwork swaying in the wind of His Spirit's efficacious presence. The Spirit of God may be powerfully present within and around us today, calling to and leading us to persons and places He wills we head towards as His ambassador. The onus is on the disciple of Christ to remain sensitive to the leading of the Holy Spirit, to be able to sense which direction His will is blowing and where He is working, and be willing to join Him there.

> CROSS-WALKING: Have you ever been surprised by "where" God has worked around you? Do you often find it difficult to sense how the Spirit of God is leading you? What are some of the clear examples of how the Holy Spirit has changed you from the inside out?

CHAPTER ELEVEN
Blindness

...I have come into the world, so that the blind will see and those who see will become blind.

—John 9:39

In John 9 we read of Jesus encountering a man who had been blind from birth. Due to poor sanitary conditions in the first century, blindness was rampant. As one's work depended on being able to see, those who were visually impaired were left with very few opportunities for employment. Consequently, the blind often resorted to begging and living off the goodwill of others. To be visually impaired in Jesus' day left one extremely vulnerable.

Today we can spot individuals in similar dire circumstances by highway off-ramps, outside office buildings, in subways, and even on the medians at street intersections. Oftentimes, such people hold a sign with a message asking for some spare change. In the first century, it was the norm to see the infirm waiting out by the various temple gates. The law of Moses had much to say about taking care of the poor and destitute. Yet much like today, the first-century world had its fair share of stereotyping as well as indifference when it came to the sick and marginalized.

One principle was known as the *Law of Retribution*, which was based on the "an eye for an eye" commandment in the Old Testament (see Exodus 21:23–27). This "law" expounded that the righteous are blessed according to their righteousness and the wicked are cursed in accordance with the measure of their wickedness (Deuteronomy 11:26–29).[13] Consequently, all of life's difficulties were perceived as judgments of one's sin. To complicate matters further, most Jews held to *three* possible explanations for one being born with some physical infirmity.

First, there was the belief that the person (who in this case was born visually impaired) was being judged for some pre-existing sin in their past life. Another view held that even the unborn were capable of transgressing *(prenatal sin)* and, therefore, depending on the sin, would be born bearing some judgment for it. Still another view had to do with *generational sin*, meaning that those who were born infirm were paying for the sin of their parents.[14]

This explains why Jesus' disciples asked the Lord if the reason the man was born blind was related to *his* sin or that of his parents (John 9:2). Being Jewish, the disciples likely asked this question with the "Law of Retribution" in mind. If the aforementioned reasons weren't enough to juggle in terms of explaining why some people were born with physical infirmities, certain rabbis chimed in and attributed natal infirmities to God judging an individual in advance for some *future* sin.[15]

The only Person whose view on this issue *really* counts, and whose perspective is entirely sovereign and true, is God Himself in Jesus Christ. Let's consider *His* response to the disciples' inquiry as to why the man in their midst was blind from birth.

---

13 "What is Retribution Theology?," Got Questions (https://www.gotquestions.org/retribution-theology.html).
14 David Jeremiah, *The Jeremiah Study Bible* (Franklin, TN: Worthy Publishing, 2016), p. 1453 (margin note on John 9:1–7).
15 www.enduringword.com/bible-commentary/john-9/

The Lord clarified that it was neither the man nor his parents who had sinned. Jesus, rather, attributed the man's blindness to the providence of God in that it occurred for one reason: *so that the work of God* (or His glory) *could be displayed in this blind man's life* (John 9:3).

That's it.

Nothing more.

Prenatal sin was clearly off the theological table. The man's visual impairment also had nothing to do with divine retribution for any future sin he'd commit. Neither did it have anything to do with some karmic reality via reincarnation!

Their Master's abrupt "fact check" likely set off some verbal firecrackers among the group of disciples assembled before the Lord.

Thanks to Jesus, they were made aware of the degree to which their leaders and teachers had been spinning them yarns of religious bunk. The Pharisees and their ilk had long spiritually misinformed those they educated (see Matthew 15:14; 23:16). Now Jesus had come and flipped many of their narratives and, in some cases, changed the script entirely! The Lord's followers would never again look at an infirm person quite the same way. It must have been tremendously emancipating for the disciples to have had their Master remove the scales of toxic indoctrination from their spiritual eyes, so as to free them up to see God as He truly is, and people, as God truly sees them.

Our story, however, doesn't end here.

After a contingent of Pharisees met up with the once-blind man, they discovered that he had been healed of his impairment and proceeded to interrogate him (along with his parents) on how he recovered his sight. Always playing the role of plaintiff in their interactions with Jesus, the Pharisees were one of three significant religious groups among the Jews during the Lord's lifetime. They were notorious for their strict adherence to Old Testament Law as well as a strong commitment to ritual purity. The Pharisees' problem was the same problem they always had with Jesus of Nazareth:

the man's healing occurred on the most inappropriate day of the week—*the Sabbath* (see John 9:13–16)! According to this particular religious sect, the compassionate actions of Jesus amounted to a giant, law-breaking no-no. Unless the person healed was near death, any attempt at healing someone on the Sabbath was prohibited.

Consequently, the Pharisees flatly refused to believe that the one who healed the man was sent by God. The sect resolved that no good Jew—especially one sent from heaven—would flippantly heal on the most sacred day of the week.

Unfortunately, just as physical blindness existed in Jesus' day, so did *spiritual* blindness!

Many people we cross paths with refuse to believe that every good and perfect gift of blessing comes from God (James 1:17). Like many among the Pharisees who rejected the presence and power of God in Jesus, there are those today who fail to acknowledge and give Him glory for the great and even miraculous things He does. Ultimately, spiritual blindness will keep those impaired by it from *seeing* the truth in Jesus. Many have tried to peg the Lord as the most intolerant teacher of all time. Yet Jesus knew more than anyone that affirming everyone's views and feelings isn't loving at all. Redirecting them to the truth, and bringing them out of spiritual darkness, is!

Nonetheless, spiritual blindness abounds (see 2 Corinthians 4:4). How, then, should disciples of Christ respond to that element of society that seems to wear unbelief like a prideful badge and touts an attitude of intolerance and hostility towards Christians and the Church?

I suggest we respond by continuing to do as the Saviour did. The Lord came to redeem sinners, not reject them. Instead of avoiding or overlooking the spiritually blind and lost, Jesus sought them out in order to rescue them from their blindness and restore them to God. Instead of criticizing and condemning them, He befriended sinners and offered to help and even heal them. When we as His ambassadors strive to minister to the spiritually blind and lost in similar ways, we unleash the heart and glory of God through our acts of grace. And never is such a ministry more impactful than when it's demonstrated in the face of religious ignorance, intolerance, and indifference.

> CROSS-WALKING: Have you encountered a situation where a "legalistic" stance got in the way of ministry by failing to see the potential for the glory of God? Why do unbelieving people so often fall short of recognizing or acknowledging the goodness of God? In what ways can we as disciples rob God of glory that's due Him?

CHAPTER TWELVE
Forgive and... Reconcile?

First go and be reconciled with your brother or sister...
—Matthew 5:24, CSB

Perhaps two of the more difficult subjects to broach in life are forgiveness and reconciliation. Jesus had something to say about each, and was concerned that His disciples' lives be characterized by their willingness to forgive and reconcile, when and where possible. The very nature of the Saviour's ministry, after all, could be summed up in the words *forgiveness* and *reconciliation*. Sinners need to be forgiven by and reconciled to a holy God. Jesus Christ made that possible by His vicarious death on the cross and subsequent resurrection. Disciples of Christ, in turn, are to reflect the heart of the One who so freely forgave them in their relationships and interactions with others.

Although reconciliation is the ultimate aim of mutual forgiveness between two people—especially two Christians—it is not always possible. Even though two believers can forgive one another, full reconciliation and restoration of fellowship doesn't always happen.

Along this line of thought, Peter asked Jesus "how many times" he should forgive someone who sinned against him. It was a valid question—one the inquiring disciple even offered to answer! It was just like Peter to always be thinking ahead (as well as out loud), to always be scrumming-up ideas and calculating scenarios—or in this case, a *number!* Peter asked the Lord if forgiving someone *"seven times"* for sinning against him would suffice (Matthew 18:21). The reason why Peter cited the number *seven* had to do with his knowledge of rabbinic tradition. Jews were taught that they could forgive someone for the same offense three times, but not four.[16]

Peter may have resolved that if he at least did better than what the Pharisees and other religious teachers were feeding the flock of Israel on the subject of forgiveness, it would come across as more than laudable to his Master. Peter's willingness to forgive someone *seven* times as opposed to *three* sounded impressively righteous to the disciple, no doubt. The Lord, however, would correct His disciple, not congratulate him. Jesus, in fact, added another *seventy* to Peter's apparently generous figure to make *seventy-seven* (Matthew 18:22)!

Let's be clear in that Jesus wasn't being literal when He stated that His disciple is to forgive someone seventy-seven times for the same sin. The Lord was saying that whoever wants to be His disciple needs to cultivate a *lifestyle* of forgiveness and not take to tabulating offenses (see Colossians 3:13). For Jesus, one shouldn't put a cap on the number of times they will forgive another person for the same sin—or *any* sin for that matter. Instead, the disciple of Christ is to forgive someone as often as they need to. Our heart is to be so big that even if someone sins against us numerous times, we are to keep forgiving as they repent. The bigger point is that this is how God treats sinners.

This doesn't mean, however, that we can always automatically trust someone again. Trust may need to be rebuilt and re-earned over time. If we value a particular friendship that has suffered as a result

---

16 R.T. France, *Tyndale New Testament Commentaries: Matthew* (Grand Rapids, MI: Eerdmans Publishing, 1985), p. 277.

Forgive and... Reconcile?

of sinful offenses and discord, perhaps we'll be more motivated to work on reconciliation. It's a testament to the authenticity of the gospel and the sincerity of believers whenever Christians forgive one another or churches abandon their fractious grievances in the interest of preserving unity within the Body of Christ. Ideally, forgiveness and reconciliation *should* hold restorative hands. That is God's plan every time. However, sometimes those hands fail to clasp in the consequential wake of sin's affect on each party.

For such a tiny New Testament letter, Philemon contains a powerful message about forgiveness and reconciliation.

A man named Philemon was an acquaintance of Paul's. It is clear from the apostle's writing that Paul led Philemon to faith in Jesus. At the time of his writing to Philemon, Paul was imprisoned. Philemon, on the other hand, was the leader of a church that met in his own home. Philemon also had a reputation for being a charitable person. Like others in his day, Philemon owned at least one slave, whom Paul identifies in the letter as a man named Onesimus.

Judging from Paul's words, Onesimus likely stole from Philemon and subsequently fled. By Roman law, a slave who stole property from their master and then ran away could be punished by death. Philemon was unaware of Onesimus's whereabouts. Had his slave fled to Rome in order to make like "Waldo" and blend himself in within that city's overcrowded streets? Little did Onesimus know that the God of his master Philemon was sovereignly arranging an encounter where the runaway slave would cross redeeming paths with the ministering slave of Christ—the apostle Paul himself!

The runaway slave was befriended by someone who knew Paul. Perhaps that same person extrapolated on the character of the apostle and highlighted his love for God and His people. Regardless of how they came together, Paul likely witnessed about Jesus to Onesimus and led *him* to faith in the Saviour. The apostle was writing to inform Philemon that he, Paul, had Onesimus with him. In addition, Paul wanted Philemon to know that his wayward slave had now become useful to the apostle. Paul was utilizing a play on words when referring to Onesimus's usefulness (Onesimus's name literally means "profitable" or "useful").[17] That said, Paul assured Philemon that it was not his intent to keep Onesimus in his company.

It was Paul's prayer that Philemon would not only forgive Onesimus and be reconciled to him, but also relate to his slave in a new, spiritual context—as a *brother* in Christ. For added incentive, Paul even offered to repay Philemon for whatever Onesimus may have stolen from him. God chose to use this venerable apostle and man of faith to broker the deal!

At Calvary, Jesus brokered God's offer to forgive sinners. There, our Lord paid the penalty for *our* offense of sin in full! While other religions instruct to dutifully "do" things in order to compensate for our spiritual deficit, the message of Christianity is always "done" (see John 19:30)! In light of the greatest of all sacrifices and acts of forgiveness, God wants *us* to forgive others as often as we need to and, if possible, be reconciled to them. If restitution needs to be made, the offending person must be willing to do so.

In the context of our worship and devotion, then, we are to examine our lives and the spiritual condition of our hearts. Jesus taught His Jewish audience that it was perfectly appropriate for them to leave their offering at the altar and seek to be reconciled with their neighbour (Matthew 5:24; see also Matthew 18:15). In his book *Forgive and Forget*, Lewis Smedes keenly noted, "Forgiving does not turn us into doormats... when we forgive, we set a prisoner free and then discover that the prisoner we set free was us."[18] Extending forgiveness to someone is one of the greatest gifts we can actually give *ourselves*. How God-glorifying it is to be able to free ourselves from a

---

17 Strong's Greek Dictionary, p. 52.
18 Lewis B. Smedes, *Forgive and Forget: Healing the Hurts We Don't Deserve* (New York, NY: Harper One Publishing, 2007), p. x.

besetting bitterness by releasing others of their offenses against us—even better, to be *reconciled* to them!

> CROSS-WALKING: Have you ever had to forgive someone multiple times for sinful offenses against you? What do you think lies at the root of one's unwillingness to forgive another? Why is the restoration of relationships between Christians so important to pursue?

CHAPTER THIRTEEN
Jesus Changes Everything

He has sent me... to set the oppressed free...
—Luke 4:14–19

There's a saying that goes, "money changes everything." Indeed, money *can* change some things, perhaps even *many* things, but it certainly can't change "everything." Such a distinction belongs not to money, but to the Saviour of the world! Only the Son of God, Jesus Christ, can truly change *everything*—in every sense of the word. We get a dramatic glimpse of this reality in Luke 8, where the possessive and destructive work of the devil in all its darkness was on full display. A man from the region of the Gerasenes (which featured a largely Gentile population), who was grossly inhabited by a mob of demons, was set free from their horrific presence within him by none other than the demon-evictor Himself, Jesus Christ.

The wicked spirits within the demon-possessed man drove him to solitary places that were far removed from society. The strength of these demons even ripped apart chains that had kept him from harming himself and others. The scene was gruesome and hopeless. But then Jesus pulled up in a boat, and *everything* changed!

The Lord took control of the demons inside the man and commanded them, at their request, to go into a herd of swine that were grazing on a nearby hill. Once inside the pigs, the demons caused them to charge towards the steep edges of the Bashan plateau that led down towards a shore where they plunged to their watery deaths. This spectacular account in the Gospel of Luke points to an overarching truth about Jesus and the far-reaching efficacy of His ministry.

When the Lord first appeared in Capernaum (after His baptism and testing in the desert), He announced that the Kingdom of God was *"near"* (Matthew 4:17). As a result of that nearness, lives were being changed and the eternal destinies of sinners were being altered!

Whenever the Kingdom of God is "near" and Jesus factors into a situation, *change*, in some form or another, is inevitable.

Whenever we bring Jesus into our relationships, those relationships begin to change. Sometimes relationships are spiritually galvanized and grow deeper as a result of the Lord being present within them. At other times, challenges of a spiritual nature are introduced to our relationships and we're forced to adapt our faith in Christ so as to be able to relate to someone who doesn't know Him. Jesus changes everything, even the ministry and witness of the Body of Christ. When Jesus is central in our fellowship, God's people are sharpened and encouraged. When He is integral to our preaching, we're confronted with our need to change the spiritual course of our thinking and actions. Whenever the ministry of Jesus is imitated in our evangelism, neighbourhoods and cities are reached with the Gospel. Whenever the Son of God moved on from one region to the next, He inevitably left change in His wake!

The residents of Gerasa got a mega-dose of the kinds of change the Kingdom of God, in the Person and power of the Saviour, was bringing about. A tortured demoniac who had been robbed of experiencing a peaceful and purposeful existence was delivered from the vise of evil and darkness that had gripped him. God's bondage and chain-breaking Son had set a captive free in sensational fashion.

Jesus is in complete control of the spirit realm; to the extent that demons—and even the devil himself—are submitted to His authority and the sovereignty of God. The exorcism and subsequent mass death of the swine, however, left the townsfolk understandably shaken and afraid. After calculating the cost of the change that Jesus had left in the aftermath of His short but scintillating ministry in Gerasa, the people asked Him to leave the area (Luke 8:34-37).

Change, regardless of the form it takes, can be difficult—even scary. We typically repel change, especially when *we* are the one being changed! Yet the Bible says that those who put their faith in Jesus Christ as their Saviour have become a *"new creation"* (2 Corinthians 5:17). The new believer is changed the very moment they accept Jesus. In fact, becoming a spiritually-reborn person is the most significant kind of change one could ever experience in this life.

Such a life is freed from the vise-grip control of the devil and the power of the sinful nature and the flesh, and empowered by the Holy Spirit to live in a God-glorifying, righteous way. But it's not like the flicking of some switch where suddenly we're changed and automatically made Christ-like. Rather, the spiritual change God wants to bring about is continuous and happens over a lifetime. It requires the continual intervention of His Spirit, as He prunes and shapes us into the people He desires we be.

In Christian theology, salvation leads naturally to *sanctification*. The term essentially refers to the process God puts us through in making us holy after we've accepted His Son. While we were still in a spiritually lost state, we certainly were not considered holy by God. Even after we become born again, holiness is something we must aspire to and grow in. Like the demoniac in Gerasa, we can come to Jesus *as we are*—spiritually darkened and in a mess of brokenness and sin—but the Saviour won't ever let us *stay* as we are. Paul referred to this as God purposing to conform us into the image of His Son (Romans 8:29).

Our redemption in Christ is designed to bring about *change;* change within us and change around us. We may feel led to change jobs or careers, or the dynamics of our work environment may change (both occurred in my life after I became a Christian). We may decide that it's appropriate to change the kinds of movies we watch, the music we listen to, or the places we go to socialize. Our view of the world will certainly change, motivating us to change how the world views us as a follower of Jesus.

God never changes things in us for the sake of change. God doesn't want to change us in order to dominate us or erase our unique personhood either. He does so in order to redeem every facet of our life and bring glory to Himself (see 1 Peter 2:9).

When I was a young Christian, I thought that God glorifying Himself in me meant that He would get what *He* wanted at my expense. I couldn't have been more wrong! Over the years I've come to learn that God never dishonours the vessel He chooses to change. As He works *in* us, He works *with* us. God is not a user, but rather uses the very desires He deposits within our redeemed hearts to fulfill our lives. If the changes God wills to make in our life bring Him glory, then they are changes that will ultimately bless us. They will be changes that are not only necessary, but ones that showcase what the power of God can do with a life surrendered to the Lordship of His Son. I'm certain that the demoniac Jesus exorcised would have agreed entirely.

> CROSS-WALKING: In what areas is God bringing about changes in your life at this time? How did Jesus change "everything" for the demoniac? Why do we sometimes resist the changes that God, through the ministry of the Holy Spirit, desires to make in our lives?

CHAPTER FOURTEEN
Ants... and the Faithfulness of God

But seek first his kingdom and his righteousness...
—Matthew 6:33

Inspiration can come from the most unlikely of sources in life—even from *ants!* Sure, we despise their infestations in our homes and we have no problem squashing these ugly little things once in a while. But according to science (and Scripture), ants are quite industrious and even inspirational! If you've ever seen one carrying food on its back or a series of them linking like freight cars as they build, you'll know what I mean. Ants instinctively know that storing food is necessary for their survival throughout the winter months.

Have you ever wondered who gave them such insight and knowledge? Do you think that even an *ant* is in touch with its Creator? I should think so!

In fact, God asks us to observe them. If creation tells us something about the Person of God, then even something as seemingly insignificant as an ant can.

> *Go to the ant… consider its ways and be wise! It has no commander, no overseer or ruler, yet it stores its provisions in summer and gathers its food at harvest.*
> —Proverbs 6:6–8

There's a parallel here for those of us who work at jobs and set budgets that frame how we allocate our resources. There's wisdom in being ant-like by "putting away for a rainy day." As the crown of God's creation, we humans are uniquely cared for by God, who promises to provide for our needs. To be sure, we are infinitely more valuable to Him than any other aspect of creation (see Matthew 6:30-33). Yet if God has given ants instinctive knowledge of the change of seasons and the need to prepare for those seasons, how much more has He instilled that wisdom in *us*? As we seek to possess the basic necessities of life, Jesus assures us that we shouldn't worry about them, but rather trust God for them.

We should establish, first, that God expects those who *can* provide for their needs to do so (see Ephesians 4:28). He has set us a pattern for working and resting. But what if we haven't managed our resources well and we find ourselves in debt? Will He turn us away? No! We may have some financial lessons to learn, but God doesn't operate like a bank or an insurance company. He's not affected by earthly, monetary bottom lines. He promises to be our all in all. Out of such knowledge, the psalmist wrote, *"The Lord is my shepherd, I lack nothing"* (Psalm 23:1).

When we come to Him for something we need, it's not like God will ever say, "You didn't save enough or tithe enough this month, so I'm not going to help you!" We won't ever hear Him say, "You didn't do your best ant-impression in saving for the winter, so tough luck." No!

God is not a legalist.

God is not a moralist either. Although the obedient life, in principle, equals a blessed life, if our sins were to mount up within a given month, it's not like He'll disown His promises to us during that stretch.

God, rather, is what I call a *faithful-ist!*

It's His very nature to remain faithful to us. In His essence, God *is* faithful. It's one of His attributes that motivates sinners to turn back to Him (1 John 1:9). *"... [I]f we are faithless, he remains faithful, for he cannot disown himself"* (2 Timothy 2:13).

However, even as we're seeking to have our needs met, Jesus teaches us that we are to make His Kingdom's agenda and living a righteous life our number one priority, above all other concerns and desires. *"But seek first his kingdom and his righteousness, and all these things will be given to you as well"* (Matthew 6:33).

Society tends to herd and mould us into a lifestyle and image of happiness that is entirely foreign to Scripture. We'll find nothing of fame and fortune in the words of Jesus in Matthew 6. We don't find Him talking about all our *wants* either. Owning nice cars and clothes and a beautiful home are luxuries in life. Perhaps many of us possess such material items, and it's not like these things are inherently negative or bad to have and enjoy. Our lack of them, however, should not be what keeps us up at night.

God is faithful to provide for our basic essentials in life. Yet He calls *us* to live a faithful life as well.

Faithfulness is a hallmark of Christian character as well as one of the "fruits" of the Spirit (see Galatians 5:22). Therefore, part of what it means to be a fruitful disciple is to be *faithful* in the things that matter to God. Jesus calls His disciples to be faithful in tending to the priorities of His Kingdom, but not as a condition for Him to be faithful to *us* (Matthew 6:33). Simply, the more we become Kingdom-conscious and focused, the more our own needs (and even our wants) will mysteriously drop to a subconscious level. As we make the things that concern God our concern, and allow them to inform our choices and impact our decisions, we'll find that He is faithfully working out all our affairs—including meeting all our practical needs. As we go about taking care of our heavenly Father's business, we'll discover that He is taking care of *ours*. In this, we'll come to possess His peace and escape the ever-squeezing (and equally ever-unproductive) vise of worrying about our lives.

Our world's economies have become increasingly unstable. The scarcity of even basic necessities is of great concern to many today. Poverty is the new tenant where the middle class—and in some cases, even the affluent—once put stakes down. Anxiety levels are soaring like never before over concerns for the quality of our lives as we grow older, over the state of healthcare and social assistance, and the affordability of housing and our ability to retire.

Thankfully, we'll never have to worry about such realities affecting God's sovereign ability (and promise) to remain faithful to us. The faithfulness of God is spiritual kryptonite to the seeming superpower of worry. I can't imagine that ants—who do not possess the knowledge of God that we humans have as the crown of His creation—worry about their supply of food or any other need. We who *have* tasted His goodness and who have come to experience His faithfulness, then, should be thoroughly ant-like in that way. As disciples of Christ, we're to faithfully seek God's will and glory and put Him first in all things. As we do, His enduring faithfulness catches us unaware. Such is a promise that even *ants* can take to their bank!

> CROSS-WALKING: Can you recall the last time the faithfulness of God in your life came shining through? In what tangible ways can you say you are seeking the Kingdom of God at the present time? Why is it so important for a Christian to have a reputation for being faithful?

CHAPTER FIFTEEN
Costly Worship

> ...everyone who wants to live a godly life... will be persecuted...
> —2 Timothy 3:12

We've heard the heartbreaking stories from missionaries and have read the gruesome details in publications from various missionary organizations. At acute points around the globe, churches and characteristically Christian villages have been burned, and pastors and parishioners tortured and murdered. Families are forced to flee for their lives and numerous believers are left with no other alternative than to meet in cavernous "underground" fellowships. Such tragedies reinforce the inerasable reality of how costly identifying with Jesus Christ can be, in a world increasingly bent on not only demonizing Christians, but silencing them.

According to Scripture, Christ followers should *expect* to be persecuted along the narrow, earthly road leading to their heavenly home. Hardship in exchange for our faith in the Son of God is more the rule than the exception. The apostle Paul wrote that suffering for our faith in Jesus has been *"granted"* to us (Philippians 1:29). Then we have the words of the Lord Himself, warning His very first followers that if the world exhibited animus towards Him, they could expect the very same treatment (John 15:18).

The Saviour saw into the future. Passages in Matthew 24 as well as in the book of Revelation reveal how widely and wildly God's people will be rejected and suffer at the hands of worldly powers before Christ returns to defeat His enemies. In John 15:18, Jesus used a word that when translated into English means "to pursue with hatred" or "detested" to describe the kinds of sentiments the world (the realm that is under the powerful influence of the devil) harbours towards God's people.[19] (See also 1 John 5:19.)

The children's television show *Sesame Street* has a segment called "Which one of these just doesn't belong?" It is often easy to spot which colour, shape, or number stands out from the others and doesn't belong with them. Similarly, Christians, as a "called-out" people, often end-up *sticking out* from their secular culture, putting them at odds with it as well. On account of their allegiance to a Saviour who makes exclusive, controversial, as well as divisive claims, the follower of Christ resembles a square peg that simply cannot be slotted into the world's round hole.

Herein lies the reality that many a devoted follower of Christ has had to spiritually shoulder, in the form of taking up and carrying the cross of their faith. On this note, the late Methodist minister and author Norman Sawchuck wrote, "We have heard it said, 'We can never wear the crown unless we bear the cross,' but for those who willingly enter into the sufferings of Jesus, the cross is their crown, and they wear it with dignity and submission."[20] Whether it's the American high-school football coach who was fired for praying at midfield after each game, or the pastor I know who was asked to leave a hospital for sharing the gospel with some inquiring patients,

---

19 "3404. miseó," *Bible Hub* (https://biblehub.com/thayers/3404.htm).
20 Rueben P. Job and Norman Shawchuck, *A Guide to Prayer for All Who Seek God* (Upper Room Books: Nashville, TN, 2006), p. 137.

many believers remain unapologetic and steadfast in their service to Christ, despite the inherent costs for doing so.

Ignatius of Loyola, the fifteenth-century Catholic priest and theologian, notably said: "If one fears men much, he will never do anything great for God. But all that one does for God in obedience to Him arouses persecution."[21] We who call Jesus "Lord" and trust Him for our salvation should not be surprised when we suffer for doing what is good and pleasing to God. When we do, however, we can rejoice in knowing that we're sharing in the very sufferings of Christ (1 Peter 3:17).

When secular society gives God's people up to misery and even martyrdom, they can take spiritual solace in knowing that there is One—Jesus—who walked that hard, lonely road all the way to Calvary. By offering ourselves unflinchingly to God, we discover the immense cost of our discipleship. Our lives, as Paul stated, resemble containers that are being poured out so that something more valuable can be put into them (2 Timothy 4:6). Joyce Rupp, in her book *The Cup of Our Life*, writes, "I have learned that I cannot always expect my life to be full… The spiritual journey is… a constant process of emptying and filling, of giving and receiving, of accepting and letting go."[22] As Christians, we are to keep our eyes fixed upon the author and perfecter of our faith: on Him, Jesus Christ, who endured intense opposition, hatred, and suffering—even the cross of crucifixion, for the sake of our eternal salvation (see Hebrews 12:1–3). What motivation to keep pressing ahead despite our earthly trials!

In our present window of time, our walk with Jesus is often harassed by worldly opposition and hostility; one day, however, we'll reign victoriously with Him in His eternal Kingdom. Jesus noted that those who suffer on account of identifying with Him are

---

21 https://www.azquotes.com/author/9092-Ignatius_of_Loyola?p=2
22 Joyce Rupp, *The Cup of Our Life: A Guide for Spiritual Growth* (Ave Maria Press, Notre Dame, IN, 1997), p. 55.

actually in a "blessed" position, for a great heavenly reward awaits them (Matthew 5:11–12). Heaven, then, holds the antidote for the world's vitriol towards God's people, and it's all wrapped up in the resurrected life of Jesus Christ. The temporal costs related to our allegiance to the Saviour will turn into *eternal* riches that are currently being held in trust for those who suffer on account of the Name that is above all names!

> CROSS-WALKING: How does the persecuted Church inspire you to continue representing Jesus in a less-than tolerant, post-Christian, postmodern society? In what ways do you feel like a "square peg" in the world's round hole? Why did so many of those whom Jesus came to save reject Him?

CHAPTER SIXTEEN
Soul Rest

Come to me, all you who are weary and burdened, and I will give you rest.
—Matthew 11:28

If there's one thing we can know with certainty about this life, it's that difficult seasons and hard times are sure to come along. Unfortunately, the abundant life Jesus wills to bless us with comes with ups, downs, and all-arounds. The ups are great. The all-arounds can be interesting or even perplexing; the downs, however, can *weigh* us down! Perhaps you're mired in some soul-sinking tribulation at the moment. In times of personal difficulty, it can feel like we're wearing a concrete necklace that's pinning us to a floor of despair. Hardship can come suddenly and unexpectedly. At other times, the clouds of a stormy season in life gather slowly and head our way gradually. In a short amount of time—even in a heartbeat—we can go from peace to pain, sunshine to rain.

The Son of God knew this better than anyone.

In an offer Charles Spurgeon referred to as "a divine prescription, curing our ills,"[23] Jesus, as the Great Physician, offered us rest in exchange for our wearied souls: *"Come to me, all you who are weary and burdened, and I will give you rest"* (Matthew 11:28).

The word I love most in that statement is "all."

Notice that the Lord wasn't saying, "Come, all of you who are *Christians"* or "all you who are churchgoers." He didn't say, "Come to me, you who read the Bible." Neither did Jesus instruct us to go to the likes of Abraham, Moses, or some other notable religious figure for some rest. We won't find Him directing us toward just any spiritual road we choose in order to encounter peace (and peace with God). He said *all* are welcome to come to *Him.* Jesus never limited His ministry in the sense that some were automatically restricted or disqualified from benefitting from it. Literally "all" are invited to come to the Saviour, irrespective of their religious beliefs or what they may think about Christianity. It's a *universal* as much as it is an *individual* invitation for us to lay our burdens down at His throne of grace.

Long before Jesus commenced His ministry years, the chosen people of God had fallen into the hands of the feared and marauding juggernaut known as the Roman Empire. The oppressive yoke of Rome lay heavily around the neck of Israel. Granted, the Jews did have a degree of autonomy in terms of worshipping, self-governance, and making a living for themselves. Nonetheless, they were modestly taxed by the Empire and were more or less slaves to Caesar and the overriding and overruling will of Rome. The Romans basically policed society and relentlessly looked over the shoulders of God's people. At one time Israel was a theocracy (God was their governing King). They had the world on a string; now the Jews were once again hanging by the strands of their submission to the wiles and whims of a foreign power and peoples.

---

23 Charles Spurgeon, "Jesus Calling," sermon delivered on June 1, 1902 (available at https://www.spurgeongems.org/sermon/chs2781.pdf), p. 9.

If that reality were not enough, the self-righteous Pharisees piled on by putting yet another kind of yoke around the necks of their people. It came via superfluous laws and traditions they established and added to the Mosaic Law. In their attempts to keep the people of God from trespassing His commandments—so as to not incur any more of His judgments—the Pharisees compounded Israel's burdens with even more weight.

For four hundred years—the time between the book of Malachi and the Gospel of Matthew—there was not a single, prophetic voice recorded nor any direction given by the Lord to His people. Although many Jews lived outside of Judea during that period, an unforeseen and unimaginable silence came over the remnant of Israelites scattered hither and thither. The onset of any tangible, prophetic hope, in the odd figure of John the Baptist, was still light years away.

By the time Israel's messiah (indeed the world's Saviour) finally arrived on the scene in the Person of Jesus, the Jews had become a pessimistic people. They'd grown weary of all the prophetic false starts and wannabe gurus in their midst. Such disappointments and dashed hopes only served to repeatedly cut Israel's messianic dreams down to realistic size. On top of that, the social landscape of Jesus' day featured a plethora of weighty burdens felt by the populace.

It didn't take much for one to be cast off from the rest of their family or society as a whole. The death of one's husband left most widows extremely vulnerable and susceptible to manipulation and even victimized by crime. If you were a leper, you knew what it was like to feel somewhere between sub-human and outright nonexistent. The poor and destitute often remained that way, while the sick and marginalized frequently had to rely on the goodwill of others just to survive. As if such burdensome realities were not enough to bear, there were also the yoke of everyone's individual sin and the pressures of everyday life in play as well.

In response to these overwhelming cares and heartaches, Jesus said, *"Come to me..."*

The Lord promised to supernaturally remove every besetting yoke from those who took Him up on His offer. Freed from such an enormous weight, those who came to Him were to then take *His* yoke upon themselves, and by that, learn from Him so that they might benefit from the Saviour's gentleness and humility (Matthew 11:29).

Gentleness and humility were scarce commodities among Israel's leadership, not to mention among those who ruled within the Roman Empire. Knowing this, Jesus offered the people something infinitely better. By instructing them to "take My yoke upon you," He meant that the wearied soul should understand that when a good and trustworthy God is really in control of their life, and when they submit to His will, they will find a rooted and contented rest they cannot find anywhere else.

It is the same restorative rest the Lord wants to manifest in the lives of those who will "come" to Him by faith today. It's too bad we often wait until one is coming to the end of their earthly life or at funerals to revisit the promises of Psalm 23, where the pre-figured Good Shepherd Himself, Jesus Christ, offers to refresh our soul (v. 3).

We're living in restless and soul-sinking times. Perhaps there are more yokes being placed around the necks of people and nations at this juncture in our world's history than at any previous time. Every facet of our society is changing, and in a whole slew of cases, not for the better. We are being told by governments and corporations that we must morph with the emerging realities of a brewing new world order. The reverberating effects of our uncertain times are being felt globally. Many are left to wallow in confusion or discouragement, while others are downright fearful at what may lay ahead; many more are experiencing the yoke of a deepening depression.

This is why Jesus' offer not only to redeem us (grant us eternal life), but to give rest to our souls in the here and now, is an intervention we cannot afford to overlook or devalue. Jesus is asking us not merely to lay our burdens *down*, but to lay them *on* Him.

Centuries before Jesus issued this invitation, a hounded and haggard David sought *and found* this exact rest in the company of the Lord:

> *Truly my soul finds rest in God; my salvation comes from him. Truly he is my rock and my salvation; he is my fortress, I will never be shaken.*
>
> —Psalm 62:1–2

Although he is arguably considered the greatest king of Israel, there were times when David was well-acquainted with what it felt like to be stripped of all his resources, and left to depend solely on God for spiritual sustenance for his wearied soul. As was the case with David, whenever we feel sacked with the weighty cares and yokes of this life it means our souls are being primed for experiencing the difference-making and life-altering power of God.

The ministry of the Holy Spirit bids to touch and alleviate those aspects of our lives that drain us and drag us down. That is why the Bible refers to the third Person of the Trinity as the "Comforter." Jesus works in tandem with Him to care for us. Who more than the Lord knows that our souls need rest from the wearing and tearing realities of living in a fallen realm? He experienced it Himself! The Saviour warned us that troubles will always go hand-in-hand with this life. Thankfully, He promises never to leave us stranded spiritually. Jesus never wills that discouragement and unrest become the norm in the lives of His disciples.

Soul rest is available to each of us, to "all" who come to God by faith in His Son, Jesus Christ. The Saviour died in order to make this rest not just temporally attainable, but *eternally* as well (see Hebrews 4:11).

The writer of Ecclesiastes noted that we were created to yearn for God; to be with Him in eternity, our soul's true home, beyond this transient world (3:11). To enter into God's rest is also to enter into His best (heaven), as they say! Nothing less than His manifest presence can fill our lives and provide one-of-a-kind rest for the soul. It's ours to experience when we go beyond merely recognizing this need to acting on it by simply coming to Him.

CROSS-WALKING: Why do you think it is imperative for us to offload burdens and find rest for our souls? How did Jesus find the kind of rest He offers us? Have you built intentional times of solitude and soul rest into your spiritual life and walk with Jesus?

CHAPTER SEVENTEEN
Rules... or Relationships?

Love the Lord your God with all your heart... Love your neighbour as yourself.
—Mark 12:30–31

Jesus fielded many an inquiry during His ministry years. Being very God, it was impossible for the Lord to be tricked or deceived into giving wrong answers. As bent as His enemies were on trying to trap Him with their loaded questions, they did so in vain. Many among the revered religious groups of Jesus' day directed inquiries at Him with clandestine strings attached. In the Lord's immaculate judgment, however, the teachers of Israel were lacking in acuity, which explained why they asked Him questions they should have been well-equipped to answer themselves!

On one occasion, a teacher of the law asked Jesus to clarify what the greatest commandment is.

One of the teachers of the law came and heard them debating. Noticing that Jesus had given them a good answer, he asked him, "Of all the commandments, which is the most important?"
—Mark 12:28

This particular teacher's motivation for asking the question likely had something to do with rating the commandments according to their significance. In Jesus' time, those who were charged with teaching the law of Moses made a common practice of categorizing the commandments as either "heavy," "great," "light," or "little."[24]

We might imagine Jesus rolling His eyes every time this sort of question arose. Who knew better than the Lord that the commandments are not about which ones are to be obeyed above the others?

The Ten Commandments are not to be understood as a hierarchy of cold and impersonal rules to master. The individual commandments were not given in a vacuum. They affect others even as they implicate ourselves. As the Master Teacher and very *embodiment* of the law, Jesus underscored the fact that the totality of the commandments deal with *relationships*—our relationship with God *and* with others (our neighbour).

Mark gives us the Lord's clarifying response to this teacher's query:

> *"The most important one," answered Jesus, "is this: 'Hear, O Israel: The Lord our God, the Lord is one. Love the Lord your God with all your heart and with all your soul and with all your mind and with all your strength.' The second is this: 'Love your neighbour as yourself.' There is no commandment greater than these."*
>
> —Mark 12:29–31

According to Jesus, if anyone intends on ranking the commandments, they'd better put loving God at the *top*, and then loving one's neighbour second.

Why?

---

24 David Jeremiah, *The Jeremiah Study Bible* (Franklin, TN: Worthy Publishing, 2016). p.1365 (footnote for Mark 12:28–34).

In a word: *love!*

If we love God with all our heart, mind, soul, and strength, and love our neighbour as we love ourself (because we wouldn't want to harm ourselves), then it doesn't matter how the other commandments rate. There is no spiritual use in establishing a level of importance for each of the Ten Commandments, because they equally rest on the unchanging principle of love. If we say we hold to the commandments, then we cannot consistently mistreat those to whom they inextricably tie us.

The principle is, if we love God as well as our neighbour, we won't attempt to break the commandments. Having said that, Jesus knows it's impossible for us *not* to break the intended *spirit* of a given commandment in some fashion. He provided for our sin in that regard, and lived a life like none other—a holy and righteous life that perfectly demonstrated what loving God and one's neighbour looks like.

The commandments, then, are the furthest thing from being individually packaged and isolated violations that are solely rule-oriented rather than relationship-centred. A love for God and for people (who are made in the image of God) is what true religious behaviour looks like and aspires to. It's the kind of *"Religion that God our Father accepts as pure and faultless..."* and that amounts to *"look[ing] after orphans and widows in their distress and [keeping] oneself from being polluted by the world"* (James 1:27). As people who profess faith in the Son of God, our godly task is to remain pure and spiritually attractive ambassadors of Christ-like love to our neighbour, whom He died for and loves as much as He loves us.

The commandments have absolutely nothing to do with simply not breaking certain *rules*. We'll be hard-pressed to find such teaching in the Bible. What we *will* find, however, are commandments that are wrapped in the context of relationships and which are meant to be lived out in godly love. It's easy to serve God and give to Him and others with a lukewarm or even cool-to-cold heart. Loving those whom we serve and sacrifice for, with our heavenly Father being *first* in that regard, is the greater point Jesus constantly strove to make. There are rules and there are relationships, but the two meld together under the will of God when the commandments are in play.

> CROSS-WALKING: Does seeing the commandments as "rules wrapped in the context of relationships" change your view of them? Why is "love" so central to the nature of the commandments and our motivation to obey them? In what ways are you actively demonstrating your love for God toward your neighbour?

CHAPTER EIGHTEEN
Losses and Gains

But whatever were gains to me I now consider loss for the sake of Christ.
—Philippians 3:7

Perhaps you can recall digging through a "lost and found" box at school in order to find an item you misplaced—a missing hat, pair of gloves, ball, or book. When it comes to *loss*, our minds tend to perceive the word in a primarily negative sense (e.g. we've lost a loved one, our employment, a precious heirloom, an investment). Losses and losing in life are so often viewed as bad. We like to get ahead, not be set back. We like to be rewarded, not reduced. Certainly, none of us desires to have our life tallied under the "loser" column for any reason!

In biblical history, there were consequences to be had whenever people refused to lose things they were never meant to hold on to.

Israel stubbornly refused to shake their idolatrous rebellion against the Lord. Lot's wife could not let go of Sodom. Achan failed to pry his fingers from the spoils of war. King Saul obsessively clung to his bitterness towards David. Judas was unable to lose his love for money and the opportunity it afforded him to betray Jesus. King

Solomon, as wise as he was, shirked any notion of turning from his foreign wives and the pagan influence they had on him and his kingdom. The rich young ruler couldn't imagine a life without affluence—at the expense of gaining eternal life. The Pharisees stubbornly adhered to their acrimony against the Lord.

However, some things we lose in life end up in the *gain* column—and then some.

I remember a story an elderly man told me about a time when he was held up at gunpoint. As a hot-dog stand business owner, he had to give his assailant all the revenue he had on hand, in addition to some of his personal effects. The incident made the local papers, which sparked a giant campaign within his community that generated more business for him than ever before. As a result, income from his hot-dog stand went up three hundred percent the following year!

When it comes to the spiritual life, losses can act as pivots that lead to better and more productive outcomes and seasons in our lives.

One of the more notable biblical examples comes straight from the transformed life of the apostle Paul.

> *But whatever were gains to me I now consider loss for the sake of Christ. What is more, I consider everything a loss because of the surpassing worth of knowing Christ Jesus my Lord, for whose sake I have lost all things. I consider them garbage, that I may gain Christ and be found in him, not having a righteousness of my own that comes from the law, but that which is through faith in Christ—the righteousness that comes from God on the basis of faith.*
>
> —Philippians 3:7–9

Paul unabashedly admitted that what he had once considered *gains* in his life (his so-called spiritual assets) actually turned out to be *losses*. The apostle Paul's impressive accumulation of learning, accolades, and zeal as a self-promoting Pharisee got him nowhere with God. In fact, Paul's efforts to secure a righteous standing with God via a works-based faith added up to a giant zero! His prior musings in legalism and self-righteousness came to be viewed as liabilities that had kept him from truly knowing God and pleasing Him.

The Greek word Paul employed in Philippians 3:7 that is translated into English as "loss" means a "detriment" or a "bad deal," and it is used only one other time in the New Testament. We find it employed by Paul when the apostle describes how cargo had to be thrown overboard in order to save the ship that he and others were on from sinking (see Acts 27).[25] It's as if the apostle was saying that all the cargo from his past life that had weighed him down spiritually and kept him from believing in Jesus had to be "thrown overboard." No wonder Paul championed the truth that to live is Christ and to die in Him is *gain* (Philippians 1:21). A marvellous spiritual reversal had taken place in the apostle's life!

We're not always going to be able to do away quickly with unhealthy things that wage spiritual war against us. Sometimes it takes time for us to realize that such things are a *detriment* to us and a *bad deal*. There are things in our lives that God may need to work on in order to square them with the character of His Son. Then there are things we may have to loosen our grip on or let go of altogether for the cause of Christ (e.g. certain possessions, habits, or comforts). Even close relatives and friends, upon hearing about our decision to become a Christian, may choose to distance themselves from us; yet new, God-appointed friends and acquaintances are sure to enter and complement our lives as a blessing from God (see Mark 10:29–30).

Whatever "gains" you amass in life, nothing is worth putting yourself on the eternal cusp of losing your very soul. We often see the world as containing everything we need for a happy and fulfilled life. Yet Jesus knows that our soul's potential to live for eternity cannot be

---

25 "2209. zémia," https://biblehub.com/greek/2209.htm.

maximized by temporal acquisitions and achievements, regardless of how grand they are.

> *What good is it for someone to gain the whole world, yet forfeit their soul? Or what can anyone give in exchange for their soul?*
> —Mark 8:36–37

Consider another loss and gain-themed line Jesus dropped on the masses: *"Whoever finds their life will lose it, and whoever loses their life for my sake will find it"* (Matthew 10:39).

In basic, spiritual terms, Jesus is saying that we only get one chance to live this life by exercising faith in Him, and *that* decision is the most consequential one we could ever make! If we miss heaven, we miss everything. Winning the world should never come at the cost of failing to prepare for the one to come. Satan essentially offered to make the world Jesus' oyster—only to find out that the Saviour wouldn't stoop to the hellish level of preserving His own life at the expense of *our* souls (Luke 4:5–8). The cross proves that the Lord did nothing for His own personal gain, but rather chose to lose His life that *we* may gain eternal life in Him.

When Jesus calls someone to be His disciple, He calls them to be dead to the kind of life that is self-fixated and self-serving. Such a life couldn't be more antithetical to the sacrificial one the Saviour lived. Along the pathway of discipleship, one may actually end up losing one's physical life for the sake of Christ, a reality captured in the indelibly selfless and timeless words of the late missionary, Jim Elliot, who lost his while ministering to the Huaorani people of Ecuador: "He is no fool who gives up what he cannot keep to gain what he cannot lose."[26]

I rest my case.

---

[26] "Jim Elliot Quotes," Quotes Gram (https://quotesgram.com/jim-elliot-quotes/, accessed 6/20/21).

CROSS-WALKING: What vices or strongholds in your life could be hindering you from leading a more obedient and productive spiritual life? Why does it tend to be difficult for us to let go of—to lose—spiritually unproductive and even harmful things in our life? Can you pinpoint losses and gains that Jesus experienced in His life and ministry?

CHAPTER NINETEEN
A Word From *the* Word!

But say the word, and my servant will be healed.

—Luke 7:7

In this fantastic portion of Scripture, Jesus' reputation as an otherworldly Person and healer intersects with the simple and yet commendable faith of a Roman centurion. Centurions were the commanders of military units numbering 100 legionnaires (soldiers). As grizzled leaders of various ranks, they doled out punishment whenever it was deemed necessary. Near the bottom on their list of priorities was being kind (at least overly kind) to God's people. Centurions were present when Jesus was on the cross. They were charged with preparing victims for crucifixion by driving spikes into their limbs. One particular centurion, after observing Jesus' unspeakable suffering and death, was moved to faith and believed the Lord to be the Son of God (Mark 15:39).

In Luke 7, a certain centurion who was familiar with Jesus' ministry possessed a servant who was gravely ill. The centurion displayed a kind heart in that he was quite concerned about his servant's health, and believed that if anyone could help him, it was Jesus of Nazareth (Luke 7:5). Perhaps this particular centurion was a feeling man—a man who was generous and compassionate and who hadn't yet grown hardened by the wiles of power and authority. This centurion obviously observed similar characteristics in Jesus. As a high ranking official, he was used to giving commands and knew his word carried a load of clout: he could tell one to "do this" and another, "do that"—and it would be done (Matthew 8:9). If anything, this centurion knew how authority worked!

Again, he must have perceived a similar authority—albeit a unique one—in Jesus. The Lord was moving among the crowds and ministering at a mesmerizing pace. In the Saviour, the centurion saw someone whose words were as captivating as they were powerful. The Bible teaches that Jesus is, in fact, the very *Word* or "logos" of God come in the flesh (John 1:1–2, 14). He is the embodiment of God's Person, speech, language, narrative, call, and rationale.[27] As Paul noted to the church in Colossae, Jesus is the *exact* representation of God (Colossians 1:15).

Obviously, Jesus was willing to physically go to the centurion's home in order to heal his servant—a *gentile,* no less. The centurion, however, felt entirely unworthy to have Jesus place even one toe on the welcome mat of his front door. Consequently, the Roman official believed that just a *word* of healing uttered by the Lord, even if from a great distance, would be sufficient enough to restore his servant's health. The centurion was saying, in effect, "Just pray for my servant right where you are, Jesus, and that is good enough for me." The exchange worked to highlight the absolute sovereignty and authority Jesus has over all creation, in that He can be all-present at all times.

Sometimes we find our ourselves in the same position as this centurion, in dire need of God moving in our circumstances. We're confronted with the same Word and promises of God, and we're challenged to believe in and stand on them. There are times when

---

27 Horst Balz and Gerhard Schneider, *Exegetical Dictionary of the New Testament, Vol. 2* (Grand Rapids, MI: Eerdmans Publishing, 1991), p. 356 (λόγος).

we find ourselves having to walk in the same faith-filled shoes as the believing centurion, and trust that just a ministering *word* from God will suffice to save the day.

Perhaps you can recall a time or times when you received a clear "word" from God, in the form of some confirmation or direction. The pressures of church ministry can be incredibly discouraging and depleting. Throughout my years as a pastor, I craved a sanctuary where I could go to be with God and listen in silence. In that space—wherever it was—I would read my Bible and then lay it across my chest as if to ingest the Word. There are precious moments in the Christian spiritual life when we hear the Holy Spirit whisper something still and small into *our* spirit, when while reading the Word of God, a sentence or verse suddenly springs from the page straight into our dank and needy soul. There are times in all of our lives when, as disciples of Jesus, we realize that God is speaking and applying the power of His Word to our life, when His well-timed grace gives us "a word" at our most desperate hour.

The book of Hebrews describes the Word of God as *"alive and active,"* reaching deep into hearts and even down into the grave to resurrect those who have died (see Hebrews 4:12; John 5:25)! It is a Word that created everything we see and which orders chaos so as to make it unrecognizably calm. It's a Word that sovereignly brings kingdoms and rulers to naught, a Word that turns hearts and lives around and even turns the tides of history. It is an unstoppable Word that is capable of meeting the cares and needs of everyday life. This is no dusty, dormant, or dead Word! This Living Word came to us embodied in the Person of Christ. Believing in the power of that Word, the centurion took Jesus *at* His Word. On account of the centurion's faith in the Son of God, his servant was instantly healed of his debilitating illness.

God has given us every reason to trust in His Word. It is a Word that, when read or heard, will never fail to accomplish the purposes for which it was sent (Isaiah 55:11). It's a Word that cuts through the powers of darkness, a Word that challenges us to *see what is invisible, believe the absolutely incredible, and accomplish what seems impossible.* It was C.S. Lewis who said that the "Christian way" is both "harder, and easier."[28] Perhaps at the crux of what makes it difficult is our need to put our confident hope in what we *cannot* see (Hebrews 11:1). Yet perhaps what makes the Christian way *easier* is found in the account of the centurion and his ill servant. There, the centurion unwittingly demonstrated how easy the Christian way of living life can be when we simply let go of our helplessness and fear of outcomes and let God's Word go to work.

> CROSS-WALKING: Have you ever received a "word" from the "Word" that carried you in the midst of a trial? What does this account tell us about the faith of the centurion? How does the outcome of the centurion's faith fuel your trust in God to handle seemingly impossible and dire circumstances in your life?

---

28 C.S. Lewis, *Mere Christianity* (San Fransisco, CA: Harper Collins, 1952), p. 196.

CHAPTER TWENTY
The Ever-Relevant WWJD

For the Son of Man came to seek and to save what was lost.
—Luke 19:10

Some years ago, the "What Would Jesus Do?" phenomenon took Christian culture by storm. It seemed like our churches were raining down wristbands with the acronym WWJD on them. Then came the WWJD bookmarks, T-shirts, sermon series, and what have you. WWJD is a clever gospel ice-breaker and theological concept. It's also a great question to apply as a biblical grid to many circumstances within the Christian spiritual life.

If one passage in the Gospels not only epitomizes the question *What Would Jesus Do?* but also answers it, it is Matthew 9:10–12:

> *While Jesus was having dinner at Matthew's house, many tax collectors and sinners came and ate with him and his disciples. When the Pharisees saw this, they asked his disciples, "Why does your teacher eat with tax collectors and sinners?"*
>
> *On hearing this, Jesus said, "It is not the healthy who need a doctor, but the sick."*

It would be an understatement to say that Jesus' actions often grated against the "norm" of what Israel's leaders held to be acceptable behaviour. By the things He said and did—and *when* He did them (e. g. healing on the Sabbath)—by where He hung out and who He associated with, our Lord turned the Jews' as well as Gentiles' perceptions of God on their heads.

Jesus always appeared at ease socializing with ordinary people, including those who were clearly disadvantaged and ostracized. By contrast, He seemed less interested in hobnobbing with the establishment and those who were deemed elite within society.

In fact, Jesus put His reputation on the firing line by mingling with individuals the likes of whom the Pharisees wouldn't have been caught dead with. Members of the sect complained to anyone who would listen that the Lord was getting a bit too comfy with people of questionable character and lifestyles. Whomever one chose to dine with was a big deal in Jesus' day; it was as if you were aligning yourself with the host. This, in part, explains why Jews and Gentiles didn't typically eat together.

Jesus chose to socialize with people whom many of the self-righteous Pharisees flat-out discarded as human beings. By asking His disciples why their Master associated with such sinners, the Pharisees were invariably indicting Jesus' credentials as well as His integrity—after all, He was popularly esteemed as a rabbi. Yet they couldn't have been more mistaken about the Lord and, at the same time, about how God views such "sinners."

The Lord spent a good amount of time with people who needed to be around Him in order to know Him—people who were morally and spiritually bankrupt, yet who often acknowledged their need of the Saviour. Jesus knew that a vast amount of the Pharisees thought they were in good spiritual shape and had little-to-no time for what He had to say. They were the so-called *healthy* the Lord referred to, who carried themselves like they had no need for the Great Physician in their midst (see Luke 5:21). The Saviour, of course, knew better.

It wasn't enough for Jesus to clarify that sinners needed to be around Him. He also informed the Pharisees that God actually filters our devotion to Him through our treatment of others. Jesus cited how the Lord rebuked the nation of Israel for going through ritual motions without possessing a truly devoted heart towards Him and goodwill toward others: *"I want you to show love, not offer sacrifices. I want you to know me more than I want burnt offerings"* (Hosea 6:6, NLT).

The Pharisees were instructed by Jesus to "go and learn" what the Lord required of His chosen people (Matthew 9:13). In revisiting their scrolls, the Pharisees would find that God is concerned with the *heart* behind any act of worship, not just with the act itself. He tunnels deep within the core of our motives and exposes them. The Pharisees could continue to go about their rituals of worship and self-righteous ways, but they weren't impressing God one iota. He desires for the worshipper to possess a heart that is in-tune with His. Jesus was thoroughly in the know when it came to just how lacking the leaders of Israel were in that department!

We can go to church and aspire to do all the "right" things in relation to the spiritual disciplines, yet still miss the mark in terms of being "Christ-like." If we fail to make room in our hearts and lives for the irreligious and downtrodden, and for people whose lifestyles and sexuality differ from ours, the outworking of our faith will fail to reach its intended WWJD potential. Jesus came not only to turn hearts back to God, but to turn the tables on those who thought they were morally and spiritually superior, yet cravenly bypassed the heart of God while attempting to represent Him.

I've known churches and church leaders that have grieved the heart of God by their lack of grace and inability to see and treat non-believing people as Jesus would. Asking "What would Jesus do?" is a great way to deal with these sorts of issues—at least, if we are willing to actually *do* what Jesus would have us do in a given situation. We're always more apt to live as the Saviour would have us live and do what He would have us do if we live out another WWJD: Walk With Jesus Daily! When it comes to being the kind of missional disciple the Lord wants us to be to the spiritually lost, a key plumbline to go by is our willingness to do what others are *unwilling* to do. Jesus made a habit of seeking out people (even notorious sinners) that His peers adamantly shunned and even condemned.

Jesus' way of making disciples was neither a new way of gaining converts nor merely a different or better way; it was and is *God's* desired way. Certainly we need discretion and discernment, boundaries and wisdom when it comes to who we befriend and share our lives with. We need to know how far Scripture permits us to go with being Jesus to the unsaved. However, each of us as His disciple must make it a priority to be *around* the spiritually sick and dying; after all, that *is* what Jesus *did*!

> CROSS-WALKING: Are outcasts, "notorious" sinners, and the irreligious a part of your social circle? How challenging is it for you to be Jesus to those around you who are searching and/or spiritually lost? Do you find yourself often asking WWJD in regard to situations and circumstances in your life?

CHAPTER TWENTY-ONE
On Our Guard Against Greed

Watch out! Be on your guard against all kinds of greed...
—Luke 12:15

There's a popular misconception—or shall we say "deception"—that the more wealth one amasses, the greater one's chance of securing lasting happiness and contentment. Yet people we run into every day could tell us otherwise. As a hospital chaplain, I've come across a good number of patients who had put savings away for retirement, only to experience later how money cannot buy everything—especially *health*. They thought that after their working days were done they could enjoy the fruit of their pensions and just live a leisurely life. Then sickness and even death came calling.

The Bible tells us that possessing a good reputation is of far greater personal value and more satisfying than even winning the lottery. In the Gospel of Luke, Jesus referred to a certain rich man, whom He called a "fool," to teach how the stockpiling of earthly wealth is an attractive deception that cannot secure one's *eternal* salvation (Luke 12:16–21).

In the Bible, a *fool* is someone who is extremely unwise. God never uses the term in a flippant manner, as we tend to. Jesus called this rich fellow a fool because he had put all his trust, peace, and future hope in the swell of his possessions. This wealthy man's land had yielded bumper crops—so much so that he wanted to tear down his existing barns and build new and bigger ones in order to contain them. This more than well-off individual kept piling up his earthly goods so that he could sit back, drink, and be merrily content, without any regard for attaining *eternal* security.

The Lord had much to say amount money and possessions, and spoke of a balanced approach when it came to managing one's wealth. He taught His disciples not to act like pack-rats in terms of accumulating treasures upon treasures while on earth, but rather to store them up in heaven, where they will last. He encouraged His listeners to follow their civil responsibilities, to give to Caesar what was his and to God what belongs to Him (Mark 12:17). Jesus, however, included an additional category we're to consider when it comes to managing our resources: *the needs of others.*

The Saviour was the most generous person ever to walk the earth. He gave much of His time and ministry's resources to others, and if that were not enough, He even went as far as to sacrifice His very life for us! In that same spirit of sacrificial living and giving, Jesus calls His disciple to a life of generosity and benevolence. For the Lord, greed is anathema to the gospel, and it has no place in the heart and life of His disciples, who surely know the extent to which God sacrificed for them. The follower of Jesus is not to preoccupy themselves with winning lotteries and get-rich schemes. They are not to make wealth and riches the sole focus of their life.

Yet many indeed do.

Professional sports athletes are making exponentially more money today than any that came before them. Oftentimes, there are professional athletes who choose to no longer honour their existing contracts and will even "sit out" if necessary in order to negotiate even greater paydays. As a result of the coronavirus pandemic, many bank accounts have taken a sizeable hit. To compensate, some people have turned to the bitcoin frenzy, where they use the coin as a financial instrument a lot like buying and selling stocks. Some cryptocurrency users have increased their wealth astronomically and continue to look for new avenues to maintain their newfound wealth and the advantages and status it affords them.

One could (and should) ask the question *how much money is enough money?* Despite the fact that consumer reports say we are spending more than any previous generation due to higher costs for goods and services, Proverbs 23:4–5 (ESV) says that we are not to "*toil*" in order to accumulate wealth, but to know when to desist. Even a very wealthy Solomon resolved that life—including all that one could accomplish and gather for oneself—is fleeting (Ecclesiastes 2:22–23).

God doesn't frown upon affluence by any means. He *is* concerned, however, with the effect that one's fascination with wealth can have on them. He wants us to be rich in giving, and not hoard and hold possessions so near to our hearts that we wind up putting our hope in them and not in Him, who promises to provide for us (see Matthew 6:19–21).

Imagine getting word that you are going to receive a nice inheritance. What's your first thought? For a lot of people, their first inclination is to think about what they can purchase or pay off, and then how much they can bank or invest what's left over. But where is the thought of giving to some helpful ministry or community outreach? Where in our plans for how we'll spend our money is an earmark to bless others in need? As our spiritual forebearers, the early Church sought especially to keep the generous nature of Jesus' Kingdom at the forefront of its ministry (Galatians 2:10).

Very little of what we've been blessed with is solely meant to pad our well-being. The Bible is wholesale in its wisdom that we are to guard against becoming near-sighted with our blessings. With a sacrificial Saviour as their lead example, then, God's people ought to be the most selfless and giving of *all* people. Generosity will always be the ultimate *greed* buster. When we see the difference our giving can make, it should become contagiously commonplace in our lives.

We all have our needs and we'll always have our wants—and many of us have varying degrees of debt as well. That being said, setting aside a tithe for God's Kingdom work and helping others around us who are in need should make the top three on our list of where to "put" our money. As we work hard and honour God with our resources, He honours *us* (Malachi 3:10–11). God not only delights in a cheerful giver, He obviously *is* one and never forgets when He sees one!

> CROSS-WALKING: Why is chasing after wealth and greed such a detriment to one's relationship with God? Would you consider yourself a generous Christian? How does the generosity of Jesus help us to guard against any onset of greed in our lives?

CHAPTER TWENTY-TWO
Being... and Not Just *Doing*

... but rejoice that your names are written in heaven.
—Luke 10: 20

Jesus was all about serving and demonstrating the fruits of His Kingdom. When we become His disciples, we're called to serve Him with our spiritual gifts and abilities. Some of God's people seem to excel at serving Him. I'm talking about those believers who are consistently fruitful at doing all they can for God by the power and grace He invests in them. In the Gospels, seventy-two followers of Jesus got a taste of what it looked and felt like to kick in the darkness and chalk up some victories for the Kingdom of God.

These disciples had no prior experience in doing anything quite like exorcizing demons. They had loads of credentials and tools when it came to the fishing trade, among other skills. But staring down Satan and robbing him of his possessions was foreign territory! Unsurprisingly, then, the multitude of returning disciples joyfully reported to Jesus that even demons submitted to them in His name (Luke 10:17). The Saviour's response always makes Him seem like a wet blanket who failed to do the occasion any justice, and surely knocked these disciples off their euphoric moorings: *"... do not rejoice that the spirits submit to you, but rejoice that your names are written in heaven"* (Luke 10:20).

We can just hear the collective sighs of the seventy-two, can't we?
Master, can we get a little more excited here?
An "Amen" would do!
How about a "Hallelujah" or something?
Lord?

Today, when missionaries bring news of God's wins and the devil's losses to our pulpits, the church cheers. When hell is stumped, the believers get pumped. More precious souls won for the home team of heaven! Joy city, right? So what was with Jesus' response to the much-celebrated report His disciples brought Him about their recent evangelistic successes?

These over-the-moon disciples couldn't have fully appreciated Jesus' response at the time. According to the Lord, it wasn't that these followers shouldn't have taken satisfaction in their successful ministry, but that they were to be exceedingly more joyous at the fact that God had chosen them to possess everlasting life.

This account reminds me of an encounter I had, as a chaplain, with a venerable minister who was nearing the end of his life. This humble man of God had a reputation for being faithful and even more fruitful in His service to Christ as a mission leader and pastor. As I sat with this older brother in the Lord, I asked him to recount one of the greatest things he had experienced in the ministry. After a few seconds of reflection, his face brightened as he replied, "That God would die for me, a sinner, and promise to come and take me to be with Him in glory."

Talk about a man who had a *Godward* perspective!

Similarly, Jesus' response to His buoyant disciples was aimed at providing them with a little *eternal* perspective.

From the get-go, the Lord was guarding His ministering followers from developing big ministry heads and losing sight of what *ultimately* mattered. Jesus would have the disciples know that their position with God was greater than their job description in the Kingdom of God. As persecuted Christians in the early Church, these same disciples would eventually grasp how comforting it was for them to know with certainty where they were headed eternally, and in whose sovereign hand their life rested.

Delighting in *being* a child of God will always put our labours for the Kingdom of God in their rightful spiritual perspective. Although the New Testament teaches that we're called to serve God with our time, talents, and treasures and be productive in our faith (doing things for Him), nothing of that nature should ever water down our desire to "be" with the Lord. This is precisely why Jesus applauded Mary's choice to sit at His feet and enjoy His company, while her sister Martha concerned herself with preparing a meal for Him. Martha, who was entirely consumed with serving the Lord, was actually missing out on something even greater (see Luke 10:38–41). The lesson here is that if there's anything more important than *doing* things for the Kingdom of God, it's making adequate time to *be* in the presence of that Kingdom's King!

Jesus frequently transitioned from doing ministry to being alone with His Father and allowing that prayerful dynamic to minister to *Him* (Mark 1:35–39). During these coveted rendezvous, the sacrificial Son of God felt held, affirmed, sheltered, and guided within His Father's presence.

When our Christian experience becomes more about serving and the usage of our gifts, at the expense of intentionally nurturing our relationship with God, we can lose our sense of acceptance and contentment as His beloved child. We should never reach the point where our spiritual life is characterized by *external* things, rather than by the *inward* reality where God abides through the Holy Spirit. The latter always informs the former. Our service to God should always be understood as a product of our relationship *with* Him, not as an adequate substitute for it.

Many sermons today reflect the urgency of our time and the need for God's people to *do* more—that is, to share the gospel more, to contend for the faith more, to go to church more and to bring our unbelieving friends with us while we're at it. As relevant as such exhortations will always be, we could use more messages from the pulpit encouraging us to *slow down* spiritually. Making adequate time to rest in God's presence daily helps to spiritually reorient and refuel the disciple of Christ and provide them with an insulating peace as a witnesses to their over-anxious world. More than doing the work of ministry, making time to be with the God we serve will aid us in becoming more familiar with *Him*, whom we're commissioned to make known.

It will always be our undeserved privilege to serve and represent Almighty God in any capacity; even greater, to simply enjoy our Creator and be able to interface with Him in the most intimate of settings.

> CROSS-WALKING: Are you able to balance "doing" with "being" as a Christian? Why does a disciple of Jesus require both? What kinds of things might deter us from keeping that balance in the spiritual life?

CHAPTER TWENTY-THREE
Peacemakers

Peacemakers who sow in peace raise a harvest of righteousness.
—James 3:18

Jesus addresses the *peacemakers* in this Beatitude. A "peacemaker" is someone who helps reconcile others to God and to one another. The Lord taught that peacemakers will also be known as *"children of God"* (Matthew 5:9). Peacemakers will be deemed children of God because *God* is a peacemaker, and those who belong to His Son are *His* children. The central act of peacemaking in human history happened on Calvary's Cross. There, God's only begotten Son and second Person of the Trinity, Jesus Christ, became sin for us in order to make peace between holy God and sinners (see 2 Corinthians 5:21; Colossians 1:20).

In the Saviour come from heaven, God issued us the greatest olive branch imaginable!

> *Therefore, since we have been justified through faith, we have peace with God through our Lord Jesus Christ, through*

whom we have gained access by faith into this grace in which we now stand.

—Romans 5:1–2

We cannot truly possess the peace of God unless we have His life alive within us through the indwelling of the Holy Spirit. In the Greek text of the New Testament, the word *peace* means "to join (together)."[29] It pictures two opposing forces that are now reconciled. In other words, they've come together after being apart. Jesus came and lived among us as the *Prince* of peace, who in a singular act would reconcile us for all time to a right relationship with our Creator. The writer of Hebrews said that on account of the *"joy set before him,"* Jesus *"endured the cross"* (12:2). The Saviour stayed the course because of the anticipatory joy that awaits our union with Him in heaven.

Similarly, those disciples who are "peacemakers" experience joy and happiness as they stand in relational gaps and assist in burying hatchets of discord and division between parties.

Our increasingly polarized culture is sorely lacking in peacemakers. We cast an eye to social media and see how some find it far easier to divide and tear down with their words—to disagree and then demonize, blame and then shame. We find it more expedient to perpetuate problems and issues rather than promote peaceful solutions. Some people seem more bent on destroying any semblance of unity than fostering harmony and preserving peace. Amid a darkening world that's trending more and more in the direction of no return from its brokenness and division, God's light-infused people are called to live peaceably with their neighbours as far as it is possible for them (Romans 12:18).

I remember having to face a bully while in elementary school. Many of my fellow schoolmates had to face the same daily punishment from the same kid. While my father was away on a business

---

29 NASB Lexicon, available at https://biblehub.com/lexicon/romans/5-1.htm.

trip, I asked my mother what I should do about the reprobate. She replied, "Ronnie, just smile at him every day." I quietly thought to myself, *Broker a peace treaty with a monster?* My response to my mother sounded something like, "Why, Mom—so he can break all of my teeth, too?"

Sometimes peace *can* be attained through acts of goodwill and humble communication.

Back in the early 1980s, then-Canadian prime minister Pierre Trudeau travelled the world in the hope of ending a global build-up of nuclear weapons. The peace initiative took Trudeau to many nations across the world. At the time, tensions between the United States and the Soviet Union were at an all-time high. Nuclear proliferation only stifled hopes for a peaceful resolution between the two world powers. With conciliatory words and peaceful intentions toward world leaders, Trudeau sought to bring about a collective awakening toward pursuing international security.

In regard to his globetrotting efforts for peace, the late prime minister opined, "A country can be influential in the world by the size of its heart and the breadth of its mind."[30]

In the face of the cold war, Pierre Trudeau chose to believe that peace was achievable through dialogue and seeking common ground. In other words, it was a *choice*.

Choosing to be a peacemaker requires *sacrifice* as well as a big heart. Peacemaking is up to you and me. The change we want to see in the world, on our street, or in our own backyard, begins with *us*! One of the prime indicators of a redeemed life, after all, is that of selflessness. Christian peacemakers realize that striving to be selfless is not the most comfortable facet of discipleship. Our ability to humble ourselves, however, so as to live in peace with others, will render us

---

[30] "Pierre Trudeau's Push for Cold War Peace," *CBC News*, 1983 (https://www.cbc.ca/player/play/1765756454).

all the more adept at mediating the restoration of relationships and other alliances.

As we return to the Sermon on the Mount, we find Jesus teaching principles that often flew in the face of Jewish thinking and tradition. The teachers of the law were still thundering that one was to take *"an eye for an eye"* and *"a tooth for a tooth"* (Matthew 5:38, NLT). The Lord countered with *"Blessed are the peacemakers, for they will be called children of God"* (Matthew 5:9). At the risk of sounding like a first-century version of a "snowflake," Jesus was simply calling His disciples to a righteousness that surpassed that of Israel's leaders and teachers. He taught them that by being conciliatory in nature and making peace with others (even Gentiles), they would be acting as *true* children of God.

Jesus was only preaching what He practiced. The Lord was diplomatic when in situations where others were deriding and dismissing Him. He was careful with those whom others treated carelessly. Jesus spoke about His enemies with measured words, even as they spoke falsely and maliciously about Him. The Lord pursued peaceful interactions with others when and where possible. He incarnated into a world steeped in spiritual arrogance, ignorance, and darkness. The Romans kept "peace" by fear-mongering and suppressing even idle threats to their power. Peace, in their Empire's dictionary, meant the absence of riots and wars. The world had yet to witness and experience the kind of peace Jesus possessed, and was more than willing to disseminate to those who were hungry to receive it.

Despite our helpless estate as sinners in a cursed world, God's love for us motivated Him to send His one and only Son to reconcile us to Him through the cross—a Son with the biggest heart of them all, who sacrificed it all for us! Those who believe in Him are at peace *with* God even as they possess the peace *of* God (Romans 5:1). It is this same supernatural peace that Jesus gives us to tide us over in a peace-challenged world (see John 14:27). With over a billion believers possessing this kind of earth-proof peace, we'd think there would be a lot of it to go around! Part and parcel of our being cross-bearers and walkers, then, is the opportunity we have to attain to the blessed ministry of peacemaking—to be carriers of and mediating agents for peace, when and where possible.

CROSS-WALKING: Do you consider yourself a peacemaker? Why or why not? Why are we "blessed" when we engage in peacemaking as Jesus' disciples? Have you ever had someone attempt to make peace between you and another person?

CHAPTER TWENTY-FOUR
When in a Dungeon of Doubt...

Blessed is anyone who does not stumble on account of me.
—Luke 7:23

From the cradle to the grave, a gamut of trials, tests, and temptations swoops into every life. Problems and pain are no respecters of persons. We could be living a godly life and consistently contributing to the Kingdom of God. We could be sacrificial believers who excel in serving the gospel. We could be prayer warriors and effective evangelists. None of these realities change, however, Jesus' warning that even His disciples will experience troubles of many kinds. Whether we're a biblical scholar or still have our spiritual training wheels on, a myriad of doubts, disappointments, and discouragements are bound to noodle their way into our lives.

We'd have thought that someone as spiritually in-tune and anointed as John the Baptist would've been able to sidestep doubts about Jesus and God's plan despite the circumstances he found himself in. John had confronted Herod about his unlawful marriage to his brother's wife, Herodias. Herod didn't take kindly to John's rebuke and proceeded to have him put behind bars. The last place anyone wanted to end up in the first century (aside from being nailed to one of their crosses) was in a Roman prison—or more of a dungeon!

John's imprisonment for taking a righteous stand was enough to cast a shadow of doubt on his confidence that Jesus was the promised One to come. The eccentric baptizer who had called people to repent as preparation for the coming Messiah, the one deemed the forerunner of the Christ who was charged with making straight paths for His ministry, the one whom Jesus said was the greatest person *"born of women,"* had sunk into a mega-crisis of faith (Matthew 11:11).

There was John—alone and likely thinking he'd gotten the short end of the righteous stick. If he was guilty of anything, it was for merely attempting to hold Herod accountable for his improprieties and violation of the law (as a king who had come from a partial Jewish heritage). The prophet Jeremiah suffered similar persecutory circumstances at the hands of Judah as he sought to hold the rebellious nation accountable for their indiscretions against the Lord. Jeremiah even went so far as to complain that the Lord had *"deceived"* and *"overpowered"* the prophet (Jeremiah 20:7).

Sometimes we suffer on account of the sin of others. The darkness of other people's lives can spread into ours, no matter how light-filled we may be. We may have remained faithful to God on some matter and yet ended up paying a high price for it. We could be living in consistent obedience to God and His Word and suddenly find ourselves enveloped by a world of trouble. Like John the Baptist, we may be striving to live a holy life—one that is consecrated to God—only to find that troubles, perhaps many, come our way nonetheless.

Have you ever had the following words with God?

"Father, I have done all you've asked of me. Why am I now suffering?"
"I've tried to do good but all it's led to is heartache!"
"All I did was tell the truth, and all it has brought me is pain!"

We're never so frank with God as when we're mired in a crisis of faith, or like John the Baptist, when we find ourselves immersed within a dungeon of doubt!

Here's where a quick and concise statement from the apostle Paul speaks to such doubts, in addressing the age-old query as to why bad things happen to good, devoted servants of God: *"...everyone who wants to live a godly life in Christ Jesus will be persecuted..."* (2 Timothy 3:12).

The apostle was speaking from experience. Paul's statement, which lacks in immediate comfort, serves as a clarion call for anyone who would dare to cross-walk. Identifying with the Name that is above all names (Jesus Christ), and remaining loyal to Him in a world that is estranged from its Creator and under the control of the evil one, can invite great challenges and even immense suffering into the life of the child of God.

We grapple with the thought that our righteous actions are sometimes not enough to prevent us from entering into times of discouragement—or worse, *disillusionment.* We tend to think in the Christian life that faithfulness on our part will be a rite of passage into experiencing joy and blessings. Indeed, the Bible is crystal clear in its message that obeying God ultimately leads to His blessing (see Genesis 22:18; Deuteronomy 11:26–28; Isaiah 1:18–20; Luke 11:28). In John's mind, however, all that his faithfulness to God's call on his life had bought him was his unwanted status as a death row inmate!

The baptizer couldn't reconcile that his faithful living before God could literally earn him a date with Herod's chopping block. Jesus, for all His Kingdom's power, had chosen to leave John's circumstances unchanged. From his dungeon's vantage point, John likely wondered, "You can raise the dead, Jesus, but you won't even consider making a jailbreak for me?" John's faith in Jesus as the promised Redeemer of Israel had reached a crossroads he probably had never imagined.

In his confusion, the jailed baptizer puts it straight to Jesus by asking Him (via messengers) a question that he thought was entirely reasonable: *"Are you the one who is to come, or should we expect someone else?"* (Matthew 11:3).

Jesus' response to John's doubts about Him provided the baptizer with a perspective from which he could see the "bigger" picture, even through prison bars.

> *Go back and report to John what you have seen and heard: The blind receive sight, the lame walk, those who have leprosy are cleansed, the deaf hear, the dead are raised, and the good news is proclaimed to the poor. Blessed is anyone who does not stumble on account of me.*
>
> —Luke 7:22–23

Jesus never promised John that *he* would be freed. Those, however, who were being held captive in their sin were being released left, right, and centre. While not making light of John's situation and outlook, Jesus gave John (as well as ourselves) reasons to actually be *encouraged*.

Even if the *servant* of God is bound, the *work* of God never is. John's fruitful ministry and righteous living would not at all be in vain—it would not go unrewarded. The One for whom John was preparing the way was indeed making redemptive inroads and accomplishing exactly what He came to do. John was not to give up hope in Jesus' Kingdom because others were now experiencing the miraculous on account of its spread.

The Saviour's response to John's doubts is His response to *our* doubt-infested queries today. Jesus is telling us, "God's got this. He is always in control. Heaven holds answers, not problems. His redemptive agenda is right on schedule. Everything is going according to His plan. You're not home yet, and I am not back yet."

When it comes to our doubting the goodness, wisdom, or power of God, the devil is always immersing himself within the details. Frances Roberts writes, "Only if [Satan] succeeds in planting seeds of doubt can he hold back the blessing of heaven among God's people and nullify their witness to the lost. So hold fast your profession of faith … there is a great recompense of reward."[31]

Heaven holds riches and rewards for all our labours and any costs related to our faith and ministries. As we persevere through life's trials, James says, *"a crown of life"* awaits us in glory (1:12)! We can keep on keeping on as faithful servants and trust God with all the rest—even our doubts. Despite our unmet expectations of Him at times, and despite His determined enemies, God's plan *is* being fulfilled. Each believer, even with their doubts dragging behind them, plays a part in that plan. We will be blessed if we do not "fall away" by allowing doubt to ensnare us to the point where it locks us up in its dungeon and throws away the key.

> CROSS-WALKING: How can doubt debilitate our faith? Has there ever been a time when you have doubted the power and goodness of God? Why doesn't God always keep us from suffering for the sin of others?

---

[31] Frances J. Roberts, *Come Away My Beloved* (Uhrichsville, OH, Barbour Books, 2002,) p. 140.

CHAPTER TWENTY-FIVE
The Ambitious Life

> ...*whoever wants to become great among you must be your servant*...
>
> —Matthew 20:20–28

Ambition. Some people have a lot of it; others, not so much. Others may be content (or not) to do what they've always done: work, raise a family, enjoy friendships, and look forward to retirement one day. But what renders a person characteristically *ambitious*? Ambition is a strong desire to do or achieve something, typically requiring determination and hard work.[32] Some people may be dedicated to their profession while having different types of hobbies on the side, without necessarily being ambitious. When we come to the two disciples, James and John, otherwise known as the sons of Zebedee (Matthew 20), they would appear to be quite the ambitious fellows!

The brothers possessed a plan they hoped would become a reality, and were armed with a campaigning mother to boot. Their ambitious (and equally outlandish) scheming shows us that James and John may have failed to appreciate their Lord's latest newsflash, in

---

32 See https://www.google.com/search?q=definition+of+ambition.

terms of the events awaiting Him in Jerusalem that would culminate in His crucifixion.

At such a crucial point in their discipleship and relationship with the Saviour, you'd think that the sons of Zebedee—indeed *all* the disciples—would have collectively agreed to dump Jesus there and then.

"Okay Lord, you go this way and we'll go that way. It was good knowing you, but we wouldn't want to be you; and on top of that, we certainly don't want to be seen with you!"

Obviously, James and John wouldn't have dreamed of walking away from their Master; after all, they had been harbouring another, rather ambitious dream!

Their mother respectfully approaches Jesus and lets the cat out of the bag: *"Grant that one of these two sons of mine may sit at your right hand and the other at your left in your kingdom"* (Matthew 20:21).

The scene takes on the feel of a hockey mom begging the coach to put her little James and Johnny on the same line as the top goal scorer. In actual fact, Mrs. Zebedee was asking Jesus something akin to allowing her sons to become two-thirds of the Trinity. (The Gospel of Mark suggests that sometime later, James and John once again approached Jesus with the same request.)

Jesus' response to this mother's extraordinary query settles all arguments when it comes to how one achieves status, even greatness, in the Kingdom of God.

First, He informs her that *she fails to grasp the enormity of what she's asking.*

We read of someone else like this in the Gospels.

Remember Peter at the event of the Transfiguration? Peter, who happened to be accompanied by these same brothers at the time, pined to stay atop Mount Horeb and build shelters for the glorious threesome of Jesus, Moses, and Elijah. Peter's suggestion was as ambitious as it was unrealistic and unsanctioned by Jesus. The Gospel writer Luke was sure to note that the enterprising Peter *"did not know what he was saying"* (Luke 9:33). Add James, John, and their mother to that list!

Secondly, Jesus challenges James' and John's ambition on the basis of His ministry as the Lamb of God and Saviour of a sin-ridden humanity.

The Lord, in effect, asks James and John, "Are you two up to the task of paying the ultimate price for the sin of others?" (In their overzealous ignorance, James and John actually said that they could!) "And what makes you guys different from all other sinners? I'll wait..."

Jesus added that the two brothers, by virtue of being His disciples, would, in fact, *have to* embrace suffering on His behalf—to *"drink from my cup"* by testifying to their faith in Him (Matthew 20:23). In that sense, the brothers *would* eventually identify with Jesus' authority in His Kingdom; their ambition of being awarded special honour in that Kingdom, however, was not the Lord's decision to make, but His Father's solely.

Lastly, Jesus responds to the mother's request to have her sons sit at His right and left hands by informing her that in His Kingdom, *greatness is associated with humble, lowly service, not privileged positions.* The Lord's comeback would have seemed foreign-sounding to His disciples' first-century ears. In their day, rulers and authorities (even their own nation's leaders) were not considered "servants" in the sense that the Saviour employed the word. Nonetheless, the disciple of Christ is to know their spiritually measured place in the world, by seeking to be *"the servant of all"* (see Mark 9:35).

Mother Teresa was once accused of not attacking the systemic problems in her society that led to the high rate of people dying on the streets of Calcutta. The late, sainted Catholic nun responded by asking for prayer that she and the other nuns would be found "faithful" and "not interfere with God's work." For Teresa, others may have been ambitious enough and even called to solve such problems, but not her. The revered nun was content to remain in the shadows of compassion and love, feeding and holding the diseased and dying in her midst. Mother Teresa left a legacy of shunning the spotlight while simply fulfilling her unique call to serve Christ in the slums of India.[33]

Heaven features a great reversal of our world's value system. Much of what's esteemed and important by our society's standards, will not be the case in our eternal, heavenly home. Jesus' rebuttal of the mother's request on behalf of her sons surely pricked James' and John's misguided, ballooning ambitions. The brothers learned that their ambitions in life were to be aligned with the nature and values of the Kingdom of God to which they now belonged.

As Reuben P. Job so aptly states, "When we can say that it is indeed Christ who lives and rules within us, we can be free of worry about the results of our driving passion."[34]

We'll never come out on the wrong side of Scripture by being ambitious, so long as we don't confuse power, privilege, and position with Jesus' definition of what it means to be *great* in His Kingdom. Humility will get us far in the eyes and heart of God. When we're content to be last, somehow God bumps us up to first. When we're ambitious to humbly serve the Kingdom of God, we attain heaven-appointed greatness. For added incentive, let's remember that even the Saviour *"did not consider equality with God something to be used to his own advantage"* (Philippians 2:6).

> CROSS-WALKING: What sorts of things are you ambitious about when it comes to your service to God and His Church? Is it difficult for you to equate lowly and humble Christian servitude with Kingdom greatness? What can you point to in Jesus' life and ministry that suggests the Lord "walked the talk"?

---

33 Dwight W. Vogel and Linda J. Vogel, *Sacramental Living: Falling Stars and Colouring Outside the Lines* (Nashville, TN: Upper Room Press, 1999), p. 80.

34 Job and Shawchuck, *A Guide to Prayer*, p. 236.

CHAPTER TWENTY-SIX
Water-Walking

I will uphold you with my righteous right hand.
—Isaiah 41:10

I recall the very first time I had to preach in front of an actual congregation. It was the mid-nineties and I was a Bible college student youth pastor at a church I was hired to serve in as a summer intern. I was twenty-nine at the time, and my only previous exposure to public speaking came when I gave my testimony in a church shortly after becoming a Christian. I had preached in class, but that was to a rather small band of fellow students—a relatively "safe" crowd. I should also mention that our sermons were of the *ten minute* variety!

The pastor I worked with for that summer placement was heading out on holidays, and he tagged me to preach on Sunday, June 30, 1996. As for the sermon's topic, I was assigned the passage in Acts 17 that details the apostle Paul's visit to the Greek philosophers at the Areopogus. *The Air-e-what-a-pus?* I remember thinking. I wasn't very familiar with the storyline of the Acts account, which only added to the challenge of preparing for my maiden voyage into the pulpit.

I would write my first official sermon and deliver it in what would turn out to be a hot summer weekend, and in a sweaty, *packed-out* church that did its best impression of a sauna!

In the days leading up to that Sunday, let's just say that this novice had more than a few monarchs fluttering around within him. It didn't help that in my early years of preaching and public speaking, I struggled with nerves as a rule. Between stammering and clamouring for air and deep breaths, I was challenged at times to look and act the part of a called and competent communicator.

As I sat in front of my finished sermon, my thoughts carried me to a particular moment in the life of the disciple Peter. I couldn't help but wonder if I was feeling (in regard to preaching my first sermon in a church) something of what may have been going through Peter's mind as he was about to step out onto the watery surface of the Sea of Galilee in an attempt to walk to his Lord. Arguably the most venturesome of the Lord's closest followers, Peter asked Jesus for the ability to defy gravity by walking on the water towards Him. (Peter asked this as proof that it was indeed his Master Jesus who was using the surface of the sea as a floor.)

Given my previous dust-ups with nerves, you can imagine that as I stepped into the church's pulpit for the very first time, I felt as if I were about to do a little water-walking myself. Sink or swim, it was my turn to "get out of the boat" and place my spiritual gifts, calling, training—not to mention my *faith*—in the sovereign and trustful hands of God.

I needed Him to provide a way for me to get through the sermon, unscathed by not only my inescapable issues with nerves, but also the greenery of my inexperience.

Prior to the start of the service that morning, someone who realized I might need to hear it read me a passage from the book of Isaiah: *"So do not fear, for I am with you; do not be dismayed, for I am your God. I will strengthen you and help you; I will uphold you with my righteous right hand"* (Isaiah 41:10).

There are many instances in the Christian spiritual life when God bids that we step out of our comfort zone and put feet to our faith—that we step out so as to walk upon the waters of uncertainty and experience His faithful hand upholding us. In each of our lives, the Lord is calling us to trust Him in this. The disciple of Christ is not spiritually cut out for living a test-free life. God uses personally challenging and stretching circumstances as if they were an anvil, to mete out our fears and shape our character and faith—a faith that the amateur water-walker himself, Peter, later described as being of *"greater worth than gold"* (1 Peter 1:7).

Peter believed that if his Lord could walk on the surface of the water, then he (Peter) could be made to do it as well. However, when the disciple switched his focus from his Master to the menacing waves that were enforcing their perilous will, he began to sink like a bag of rocks. In other words, once Peter switched his focus from faith to fear, he sank!

Failing to trust God in the midst of life's acutely challenging moments can leave the believer flailing spiritually—like Peter, floundering in a sea of panic. Fear seeks to wag the dog of our faith. Like faith, fear can be incredibly contagious. It can spread to every facet of our being, from our head to our hearts, and show up in our attitudes and actions. Every day the disciple of Christ must choose which will reign in their life: faith or fear. Our faith in the One (Jesus) who overcame the world—and even walked on its water while He was at it—is designed to inoculate our fears and render them anti-viral. Spiritual fruit tends to hang "out on the limb," to extend the analogy. If we're to grab hold of it, we need to be willing to not only step out on that limb, but also to trust God if that limb begins to give way. We need to believe that He will catch us, just as Jesus did Peter!

In the spiritual sense, to water-walk means telling the water how much bigger its Creator is. We can confidently step out of our boats of security and onto the waters of uncertainty, knowing that it is God who made those very waters. It is He who is manufacturing the very circumstances He appoints us to trust Him *with* and *in*.

The same lifesaving hand that plucked a sinking Peter from the sea strengthened and upheld me during my first Sunday in the pulpit. I may not have physically walked on water that morning, yet spiritually speaking, my feet were wetter than ever before!

We're all in the same boat when it comes to being guilty now and again of taking our spiritual eyes off the One who calms the storms, and fixing them on tempests threatening to take us down along with our faith. We all have a little bit of Peter in us that way. God is continually calling us to trust Him by stepping out in areas of our life where we're prone to stepping back. As a venerable preacher I heard once put it, "There is nothing we cannot walk towards with Jesus leading the way." He is the same One who bids to turn us from being mere toe-dippers into full-fledged water-walkers. If we're willing to step out, He's more than able to keep us afloat.

> CROSS-WALK: Are there areas of your life that you find difficult to trust God with? What keeps you up fearing at night, as opposed to sleeping in faith? What precisely is God bidding you to get out of your boat of complacency and walk towards?

CHAPTER TWENTY-SEVEN
This Court Is Now in Session!

Do not judge, or you too will be judged.
—Matthew 7:1

Chapter Seven of Matthew's Gospel contains one of Jesus' most misunderstood teachings. We've all heard someone say, "We shouldn't judge" or "I'm not going to judge" and even "Stop judging me!" But can we, in all cases, simply say, "Don't ever judge"? Is that *really* what Jesus was conveying to His listeners? He knew we'd stumble on this issue—that we'd squabble and falter over how to handle the sins of others, let alone our *own*. Perhaps this is why we tend to get a bit touchy and nervous whenever our eyes catch this particular segment of the Sermon on the Mount.

Each of us, regardless of our station in life and whether we're a follower of Jesus or not, can see something of ourselves mirrored in the words spoken by our Lord in Matthew 7:1–5. It's quite natural for us to share our opinion about something or someone, even to the point of passing judgment. Social media platforms have become virtual kangaroo courts, where judgments are rendered fast and furious. No matter how critical or fair and constructive our opinions of things and judgments of others may be, none of us prefers to be on the receiving end (*being* judged).

Each Christian *must* make a judgment call as to how they will align their biblical values and faith with the norms and currents of their secular culture. If a law or trend in society asks me to do something that may compromise my allegiance to Jesus and hurt my testimony, I have a choice to make, a choice that forces me to make a *judgment* call. First and foremost, I must consider whether the action in question is biblical or not. Is it spiritually advisable or harmful? Is it beneficial or detrimental to me and others? The disciple of Christ must always be ready to weigh what he or she believes to be righteous against what is not, in order to make the best and wisest (biblical) decision.

Surely the Lord doesn't call us to check our spiritual faculties at the door before entering any room! At no time does the greater teaching of the Bible direct us to suspend all critical thinking when it comes to those things that affect us spiritually, as God's holy people. He didn't create us to be religious simpletons that are ignorant and content to let sin be sin in our lives or in the Church. Having said that, Jesus' disciple is not to think or act like he or she is the *ultimate* judge either. There's only One who is capable of rendering perfect (and final) judgment, and He is sinless and holy: *Almighty God* (see James 4:11–12). Motives, ministries, and the hidden things of our hearts and lives will be examined in full and exposed by God at an appointed time (see 1 Corinthians 4:5).

Let's consider for a moment, then, what the Lord *did not* mean by His words, *"Do not judge..."*

Jesus was not saying that we are *never* to render a judgment on anyone or anything. Our Lord did not mean that we're to look the other way when it comes to sin and injustice, to things that quench and grieve the Holy Spirit and which threaten the witness of the Church. Why, after all, do we have laws, courts, lawyers, and judges?

Each one of the aforementioned is biblical. Why does the Church, for that matter, have representatives governing and overseeing its affairs?

It's best to see Jesus' teaching on judging others as being a *guideline* that helps us assess and address what is spiritually true or false, biblical or unbiblical, and how to confront sin in the most cautious, wisest, fairest, and gracious of ways.

Some people are just poor judges of other people and their character; others possess either a speck of short-sighted sawdust or even a hypocritical plank in their eye as they attempt to pass judgment on something or someone. That was the Pharisees' game. Members of the sect typically came down hard on their fellow Jews for not doing something they themselves were unwilling to carry out. The best person to hold us spiritually accountable, then, is not the one who is struggling with the same issues as us (see Romans 2:21–23)!

Sin mars our discernment. The measure we use to judge others' actions will likely be the one they use to judge ours (Matthew 7:2). We need to be willing to do a little self-critique and introspection before we go about critiquing someone else's life. Some people are overly critical of others and are always pointing out the faults they see in people. Jesus frowns upon any propensity we may have to pick at and pick on someone for their spiritual shortcomings. Prayerful self-awareness and an attentiveness to our motives can be sorely lacking when we engage in judging the actions of others.

Jesus permits us to intervene when another Christian is caught in sin. Paul says that it's our brotherly and sisterly privilege to assist in restoring a fellow believer to righteous living (Galatians 6:1). Leaders in the Church, especially, need to be able to deal with sin in the Body of Christ. Some situations call for the elders, in a biblical and loving manner, to spiritually care for and direct (discipline) a brother or sister in the Lord. When church leaders implement consequences for sin, however, they're not to do so harshly nor by using condemning language. The goal of disciplining sin in the Church is always *restoration* to full fellowship.

We can *look* right, *sound* right, and *think* we're right when making judgment calls, and yet be entirely off-base and wrong. We're dealing with people's lives and reputations. We must be care-*filled* if we're going to be care*ful* when it comes to handling the sin of others. Jesus knows what it feels like to be falsely accused. His crucifixion was the greatest injustice known to humanity. He was judged unfairly and hypocritically. He knows what it's like to be on the receiving end of judgments that have nothing to do with truth, seeking understanding, or reconciliation. Let's not make these same mistakes.

CROSS-WALKING: What's the difference between being *judgmental* and judging according to biblical standards? Do you find it challenging to live out Jesus' teaching on judging? Has there ever been a time when you felt you were judged unfairly?

CHAPTER TWENTY-EIGHT
Second Chances

Jesus said, "Feed my lambs."

—John 21:15–19

Have you ever been let off by a police officer who cancelled a ticket with your name and traffic violation written on it? Have you ever been given the chance to right a wrong you've done to someone? How about the chance to take a make-up exam or another shot at convincing an employer that you're the right person for the job? We love second chances in life—even *third* chances are nice to have! To be able to redeem ourselves for blown opportunities, past mistakes, and errors in judgment is a precious commodity in life that most of us would be all too eager to capitalize on.

Most of us would jump at a chance to do something better than we did the first time. I've had such chances, and you likely have as well. Once again the disciple Peter comes to the fore as someone in the Gospels whose life was defined by a *second chance*. None of us would dream of openly denying our faith in Jesus Christ. In his heart of hearts, the disciple likely thought that if push ever came to shove, he could and *would* stand up and be counted for his Saviour. Peter's pratfall on the first century world's stage—that perhaps made him more famous for what he got wrong than what he got right—was not simply the product of some miscreant trying to pass himself off as a disciple, as if something like that would have fooled the Lord!

By all indications, Peter had a cocky streak running through him; after all, it was he who *promised* never to forsake the Lord: "Jesus, even if everyone else leaves you, I never will… You can count on me… I'm all in!" (See Matthew 26:33–35).

However, Jesus, being Jesus, knew that despite any good intentions Peter possessed, His plucky follower would experience a self-manufactured glitch in his commitment to Him. Jesus *warned* Peter that the disciple would, in fact, deny Him—not once, or even twice, but *three* times before a certain rooster could be heard crowing (Matthew 26:34). That, of course, is exactly what happened. When the heat of reprisal for identifying with the Lord had been turned up, Peter wilted like a sun-soaked plant. Fearing that any admission of allegiance to Jesus on his part would be ground zero for him, Peter did his best to convince people that he didn't even know his Master. Immediately following his denials, however, the Gospels tell us that Peter *"wept bitterly"* (Luke 22:62).

If someone would have told Peter in that moment that his Master would not only forgive him but also turn the broken disciple into a pillar of leadership in His Church, I surmise Peter would have thought they were underestimating the gravity of his sin.

This takes us to the last chapter of John's Gospel. The scene is poignant for how it memorializes Peter's reinstatement—or *second chance.*

The disciples had been out on the water all night, fishing. By dawn's early light, their nets remained empty. As they approached the shore, they spotted a distant figure on the beach (whom they failed to recognize as being Jesus) cooking some food. This person seemed to be omniscient, knowing where the fish were residing, and proceeding to direct the tired and skeptical disciples to that location. Sure enough, the disciples subsequently hauled one hundred and fifty fish ashore!

When Peter realized that this clairvoyant figure was in fact *Jesus,* the disciple began his mad dash through the wall of water separating him from the Lord. Peter couldn't reach the banks where the Lord sat waiting fast enough. Perhaps they would have time together to address the disciple's denial of his Master. It's also possible that Peter had already repented to the Lord and the disciple was simply overjoyed to see Jesus again. Whatever the case, it's as if his Master said to Peter, "Let's take a walk along the beach. I've got some things I want to chat with you about." Through a series of three pointed questions He directed solely at Peter, Jesus gently restored His disciple to the ministry He had marked out for him (see John 21:15–17).

Although this was the third time the Lord appeared to His disciples after His Resurrection, Peter came to know it as his *second* chance at making things right with his gracious Master, and forged ahead with a new lease on his ministry life.

What's our takeaway here?

Firstly, we must truly grasp the capacity God possesses to extend grace to us. As I often like to say: *God is gracious with a capital G!* In fact, I believe God is more gracious than His people sometimes make Him out to be. The late country-and-western artist Johnny Cash used to go on drug- and alcohol-induced escapades. Although he started and finished his life well, spiritually, the music legend came close to ruining it on multiple occasions. Yet Cash still stands as an example of a person who discovered that by His enormous amount of grace, God grants second chances. Without question, the cross shows us just how serious Jesus is about our sin and how it can separate sinners from God forever. What's also indisputable from the Gospels is the crucial emphasis the Lord puts on *grace,* in that He is equally serious about forgiving us and restoring us to God and to righteous living. Why else would Jesus instruct us to keep forgiving someone no matter how often they sin against us? He never gives up on anyone, and neither does He want us to.

Secondly, God *uses flawed people* (sinners) to serve Him. He uses our failures and the fallout from our rebellious sins (whatever degree they may be) to motivate us toward obedient, godly living and spiritual renewal (see Psalm 25; 51). He shames the proud with His willingness to use the ill-esteemed and lowly (see 1 Corinthians 1:27–29; also Daniel 4:17). Why else would the Lord forgive the woman caught in adultery and give her another chance to honour God with her life?

Lastly, our spiritual shortcomings and misgivings can be *redeemed* by God and used as part of His plan for our life. Did Jesus dump Thomas for doubting Him? No. Did Jesus dispose of the Sons of Thunder (James and John) for wanting to call down fire on the Samaritans for disrespecting their Master? No! Did the Lord hold a grudge towards all His disciples for deserting Him at the cross? Again, no. And as we see from John 21, neither did Jesus discard Peter as a consequence for the disciple having denied Him three times.

Jesus simply asked Peter if the disciple *loved* Him above anything or anyone else. The Lord didn't brow-beat His tender follower and then warn him *not to do it again*. Jesus knew Peter's heart and knew he was a keeper for His Kingdom's work that was yet to come. Thankfully, God issues new days and new ways for us to be involved in His work, as we resolve our misgivings and sin at His throne of grace (Hebrews 4:16). He *can* and *will* use those of us who are seeking to cash-in our umpteenth chance. He can and will use those who've experienced their fair-share of personal failures and subsequent rooster crows. If He is the God of the "eleventh hour," then He is also the God of the second chance. Believe it and take Him up on it!

> CROSS-WALKING: When was the last time you yearned for a "second chance" from God after having let Him down in some way? Can you think of flawed biblical figures whom God used mightily? What kinds of thoughts and emotions

might have flowed through Peter's mind and heart after Jesus not only forgave the disciple, but reinstated him?

CHAPTER TWENTY-NINE
"Scoring" for Jesus

Therefore go and make disciples of all nations...
—Matthew 28:19

Canadian hockey legend Wayne Gretzky is credited as once saying "You miss one hundred percent of the shots you don't take."[35] I think the five-time Stanley Cup champion meant something to the effect that if he didn't attempt to shoot the puck, he couldn't expect to score any goals. But score goals is what Gretzky did—in abundance, on his way to setting many a record in the National Hockey League. There's a lesson to be gleaned here from the words of the so-called "Great One." In the game of hockey, *shooting* the puck and taking aim at the net (a shot on goal) doesn't always lead to goals being *scored*, of course—but the latter cannot be experienced without first engaging in the former!

Goals of another sort that we associate with our lives are often there for the having if we'd only... well... take the *shot!* Some of the personal goals we set in life may be highly achievable and realistic; others may be literal *long*-shots. Setting goals is a good practice in life. Our desire to set goals doesn't mean that we're overconfident and

---

35 Available at https://www.sportsfeelgoodstories.com/best-wayne-gretzky-quotes/

getting ahead of ourselves. It doesn't mean that we're going against the wisdom of Scripture that instructs us to take life day-to-day and not boast about our plans for tomorrow (James 4:13–17). Goal setting is a positive way to live our lives with motivation and vision. In fact, some of our world's pioneering personalities and visionaries possessed dreams that later became goals that eventually revolutionized industries and/or even modern life in general. They took their shot and they scored!

We shouldn't be surprised, then, by the fact that Jesus Himself set goals for His ministry and then passed those same goals on to those who would serve Him in the world (John 14:12; 15:27; 17:18). The Lord left His future pioneering leaders of the early Church some high-stakes goals to take aim at, shoot, and score. This same game plan has been passed on through every century and generation of the Church, and it will continue to be up to the very day Jesus returns. We're talking about the kind of evangelistic goals that every believer in Christ would love to see lodged within the nets of their efforts as they serve the Kingdom of God.

Similarly to how athletes are drafted by sports teams to play in professional leagues, Jesus drafted His disciples to be on *His* team: *Team Heaven*. The family of God is like a "team" in the sense that each member plays a necessary role in advancing the gospel—with the ultimate goal of winning souls to Christ. To be exact, God has a game-plan for each and every person who has trusted His Son for their salvation. It's found in the last chapter of Matthew's Gospel. From the "Great One" to the Great Commission!

In one of Jesus' last words of instruction to His disciples before He ascended back into heaven, He unveiled the goal and game-plan God had for their lives:

> *Then Jesus came to them and said, "All authority in heaven and on earth has been given to me. Therefore go and make disciples*

of all nations, baptizing them in the name of the Father and of the Son and of the Holy Spirit, and teaching them to obey everything I have commanded you. And surely I am with you always, to the very end of the age.
—Matthew 28:18–20

A quick overview of the Commission's game-plan reveals that the Lord *expects* that we will share our faith with others who don't know Him as Saviour. Our Lord expects us to not merely root for the home team of heaven, but to get in the game and light up the scoreboard of heaven ourselves! He expects our lives to be an advertisement for the love and grace of God, to be exhibits showcasing the power and glory of God. Followers of Jesus Christ don't merely share the good news of the gospel, they *embody* it! When a Christian shares their faith, they're invariably sharing their lives as well.

In a troubled world barrelling with abandon towards the Great Tribulation, each disciple of Jesus carries with them a goal to fulfill and a game-plan to carry out in the form of an even greater *Commission*. It's good news that is too good not to be true and not to be *shared!* When Christians stand before God's throne at the end of their earthly lives, they will have to account for what they did with the knowledge of God and spiritual gifts they possessed. Believers of all ages will have their earthly works scrutinized at the judgment seat of Christ (1 Corinthians 3:12–15; 2 Corinthians 5:10; see also Ephesians 2:10).

The Lord will examine whether we followed His game-plan by doing what we could to fulfill the Great Commission.

Did we live as if to express the love, grace, power, and glory of God? Did we attempt to score evangelistic goals for Jesus? In other words, did we share the good news of the gospel and point people to Christ? Did we attempt to plant seeds in the lives of the spiritually lost? Did we pray for those we wanted to see in heaven? Did we maximize our salt and light qualities and work to preserve truth in the world?

Every child of God is called and equipped to live a spiritually productive (fruitful) life as a testimony to the world. Part and parcel of this is the believer's call to a personal mission field, where they move from knowing Jesus to *making* Him known in their spheres of influence. The goal is for one more soul to escape having to spend a horrible eternity without God, and be tallied on the scoreboard of heaven and eternal life instead!

Similar to the game of hockey, where if we don't take aim at the net we'll never score a goal, if we don't make it our personal responsibility to do our small part in helping to fulfill the Great Commission, we'll fall short of the central goal Jesus set for us as His disciples (Luke 5:10).

At this late hour in our world's history, when bad news seems to be the only news we're hearing, people are looking for anything that resembles tangible hope to hang on to. More than ever, people from every nation and corner of the earth are collectively discerning that they're in need of rescue. Our economically and socially torn and divided cities and communities are desperately longing for restoration and healing. Has there ever been a time when our society has been this vulnerable—or more primed for those who know the good news of the gospel to *be* that to them?

Personal evangelism will always be that facet of our discipleship that is less than comfortable and convenient. Jesus never said that scoring for Him would be as easy as shooting on an empty net. Fulfilling the Great Commission is an exercise in overcoming obstacles that stand in the way of our evangelistic goals—those related to our own fears and feelings of inadequacy, and those pertaining to the reaction of the people we share the gospel with.

I got a taste of that reality when I got into church planting. Whether our steering and planning committees were taking the Good News door-to-door or sharing our vision at a town hall, bringing the gospel to any neighbourhood can be like stepping onto a battlefield where God's people have no choice but to engage in spiritual warfare. Who knows better than Jesus that Satan claims ownership in territories where the Saviour sends us with the game-plan of the Great Commission?!

Learning to shoot, let alone score for Jesus, takes training and practice. It takes a bit of creative play-making, capitalizing on opportunities, not to mention the spiritually indispensable footwork of prayer. I've yet to come across many "all-stars" when it comes to sheer giftedness in being able to score for Jesus. Hall of Fame athletes in any sport do not come a dime a dozen. Even so, we're not reaching for fame or to make a name for ourselves, only to remain faithful at taking shots at proclaiming the Name above all other names.

There remains no shortage of people around us who are without God and without hope in the world. Whether those around us choose to say "yes" to Jesus or "no," each of us, as a disciple of Christ, bears the same goals and game-plan He possessed and passed on to us. As it was for the "Great One" in hockey, we'll miss one hundred percent of the shots we *don't* take at sharing the Good News of Jesus with someone who needs to hear. With the power and blessing of God behind our "shot," we have nothing of eternal value to lose by taking it. Those we do share the gospel with, on the other hand, have eternity to gain!

> CROSS-WALKING: Are you able to say that you actively play a role in discipling new believers? Do you feel you have grown more adept at sharing your faith, "taking shots" for Jesus? How does it feel when you are able to tell others about your faith?

CHAPTER THIRTY
Sign o' the Times

All these are the beginning of birth pains.

—Matthew 24:8

To say that we are living in uncertain times is the greatest of all understatements. How much closer can the Bulletin of the Atomic Scientists' "doomsday clock" get to striking midnight?[36] The global pandemic that struck our planet in the form of COVID-19 in 2020 unleashed a frenzy of so-called "conspiracy theories," while revitalizing discussions about end-time prophecies and scenarios within Jesus' church. The emergence of mandated COVID vaccines and the requirement of vaccine passports and "QR" codes for travelling and accessing certain services has triggered the imaginations of many Christians, leading them to consider whether we're experiencing the scheming build-up to the establishment of the "mark of the beast" system, where one's ability to participate in society will require them to take the mark of the antichrist (Revelation 13:15–18).

Then there's the totalitarian actions of certain governments in terms of their overreach against law-abiding citizens and the increased censorship of social media users by Big Tech. Add to

---

36 See https://thebulletin.org/doomsday-clock/

that the prospect of digital IDs being instituted along with a social credit system, the emergence of the World Economic Forum with its agenda to install "The Great Reset," and the likelihood of that spawning a "new world order" that will bring every facet of life under its dictatorial control, including a universal financial currency and system and eventually, regulations on even religious freedoms and expressions, and suddenly we appear to have a prophetic powder-keg that is nearing detonation on our hands.

Whatever was perceived to be "normal" or predictable about our lives, indeed the world, is not making a comeback. At this rate we won't be able to count "in spades" those who feel just as optimistic about our world's future as they once did. We've pretty near lost all confidence and trust in our politicians and in the policies they posit that are aimed at bringing about hope for better tomorrows. The idea that humanity is trending upwards morally, and is more aware and informed (or "woke") than any previous generation, is being exposed for the mythical lie that it is.

Although we could never have conceived a time such as this, the same could not be said of the Son of God. In Matthew 24, Jesus, in conversation with His disciples, foretold events pertaining to what the Jews would have understood as a time called the *end of days* that is cited several times in the Tanakh (Hebrew Bible), in addition to parts of the Old Testament (e.g. Jeremiah, Ezekiel, and Daniel).

In one sense, the events the Lord prophesied about would occur *during* the lifetime of His first followers; their *ultimate* fulfillment, however, would take place at a future time. The disciples were like us in that they too looked at their world and wondered when the end of days would transpire. They too were concerned with looking for signs, which was a very Jewish way of discerning the end of the age. Naturally, then, they were also fixated on the *timing* of their Master's return to earth. Therefore, most of Jesus' prophecies in Matthew 24 concentrate on the various "signs" the Lord said would precede His return to the world and the eventual end of the age.

If the end of days and the age of humanity is close upon us, can we know with certainty when it will take place? It's not a modern question, but rather one that's been asked for centuries. The question was asked when the ancient prophets walked the earth. Today the question of when the end will come is a closer-than-ever reality blaring on the radars of countless of expectant Christians. In fact, for many of God's people across the world, Jesus can't come back soon enough!

We know from the Lord's words in Matthew 24 that near the end, a great deception and delusion will take place throughout the world. Jesus said there will also be wars and rumours of wars. (The Russian invasion of Ukraine and the subsequent war between the two countries that began in early 2022 reignited fascination with this particular prophecy.) In addition, Jesus noted that there will be physical signs like famines and earthquakes in various places, which would constitute the *"beginning of birth pains"* (24:8); in other words, such signs will set the earthly stage for what's yet to come.

Furthermore, Jesus said that kingdoms would rise up against other kingdoms and that the world would unite to turn against God's people. The Lord also warned that false prophets and messiahs would run rampant and make their bogus claims. Still another end of the age "sign" He left us was increasing wickedness on the earth. The Temple would be desecrated—a sign that was prefigured by the actions of the pagan king Antiochus IV in 167 BC, and that will ultimately be fulfilled at the hands of the antichrist during the coming Great Tribulation.

Jesus wrapped it all up by insisting that the exact day and hour of His return *cannot* be known (Matthew 24:36). Many individuals have attempted to put a date on Jesus' return and even gathered followers to themselves, only to be exposed as the fraudulent prophets they were. It's easy to get caught-up in end-time hysteria and guessing games about potential scenarios and the identity of the antichrist. Never has the prophetic term "Gog and Magog" been on the tongues of more believers or more popular in pulpits than it is today.

One thing I believe all of God's people *can* agree on is that we *are* getting ever-closer to the rapture of the Church and the events that will ensue, leading to Jesus' Second Coming and the battle of Armageddon. We are a world in a tailspin, where biblical prophecies appear to be converging at a rapid and spiritually dizzying pace. As disciples of Christ, we ask ourselves: how much more evil needs to happen? How much more suffering has to take place? How much more time must be given to those who've yet to repent to, in fact, *repent*? How much longer until we fly?

It would be fair to say that the signs Jesus highlighted in Matthew 24 that will precede His return have *always* been with us. The Lord was likely referring to the fact that there will be an increasing amount and more intense experience of these signs and prophecies at the end of the age. Nonetheless, Jesus redirected His disciples' focus from entertaining too many particulars in terms of the *signs* preceding the rapture and His Second Coming to simply being *prepared* for the event.

The Saviour is concerned with *how* His disciple is to live *while* they await His return, and it has everything to do with remaining steadfast as a cross-bearing and walking people of God.

> *Therefore keep watch, because you do not know on what day your Lord will come… So you… must be ready, because the Son of Man will come at an hour when you do not expect him.*
> —Matthew 24:42, 44

Throughout the Gospels, Jesus calls His disciples to remain sober and alert in preparation for the hour of His coming. That same urgency of preparedness is repeated by the authors of the New

Testament. Even the first believers to follow Christ got caught up in baseless rumours concerning the rapture; some even became mired in idleness on account of believing that the Lord's return was about to occur. Others falsely believed that it had already happened and they had been left behind (2 Thessalonians 2:1–3; 3:6).

We need to be living as if the Lord were coming back *today*, and not get bogged down in predicting *when*. We're certainly not to rest on our spiritual laurels, thinking that we needn't do much more with Jesus right at the door, as it were. I'm reminded of what the angel said to the disciples after they witnessed Jesus ascend into heaven: *"why do you stand here looking into the sky?"* (Acts 1:11). Christians are surely not to neglect anticipating the rapture of the Church. In the spiritual sense, we're called to be watchers of the skies (see 1 Thessalonians 5:6). Our Saviour wants us to be equipped to discern the biblical signs leading up to His imminent return (Luke 21:28). They serve to remind us that the event is close at hand. Yet merely "standing there" until the Lord returns can produce all sorts of spiritually unproductive habits. Complacency has no place in our yearning for Jesus' Kingdom to come. We're to be ready, with our Kingdom lamps topped up with light and life-giving oil!

We're called to live the kind of righteous Kingdom life that keeps going about our heavenly Father's redemptive business. We're to be "caught in the act" of serving His Kingdom when Jesus returns. Let us be cognizant of living for Him each and every moment, because the Lord could return for His Church at *any* moment. The day of Jesus' return has long been on its glorious way. For now we must endure through the signs that point to that very hour.

CROSS-WALKING: Considering the signs of the times, do you find yourself increasingly preoccupied with "watching the skies"? How can Christians remain ready for Jesus' return? Why do you think God's people tend to get so caught up with end time events and preaching?

CHAPTER THIRTY-ONE
Coming to the End of Ourselves

My Father... may your will be done.

—Matthew 26:42

While in Bible college I took a course on the Gospel of Matthew. When our professor lectured on the account of Jesus in Gethsemane, he noted how provocatively the Gospel writer described the event. According to Matthew's original language, what we have is a picture of the Son of God falling prostrate, as if overcome by grief or even terror. Acting out under the influences of extreme stress and anxiety, our Lord likely looked as if He'd had "a few too many." At Gethsemane's desperate hour, Jesus volunteered that His soul was grievously overwhelmed to the point of death (Matthew 26:38). Before He would even make it to Calvary, the Saviour was feeling death's cold encroachment within Him. For all His righteous intentions and eternal purposes, the Son of God had finally come to the end of Himself.

In that singular moment, Jesus' whole person—spiritually, emotionally, and physically—was collapsing under the crushing reality of having to bear, and then die for, the sin of the world. Each of us has likely experienced moments when we felt as if we had reached the *end of ourselves*, when we felt as though we've played our last card and found ourselves devoid of options, ideas, and time, in terms of solving some deep, personal issue. It could have had to do with a crisis involving our health or financial well-being. We might have come to the end of ourselves in terms of what to do about a family matter or a relationship. Perhaps we tried to take matters into our own hands by plotting and planning, only to find roadblocks to our goals. Perhaps we're all too familiar with what closed doors, dead-ends and no-way-outs feel like.

Many of us have experienced times when we felt as though all our systems had failed and we were powerless to bring about an outcome that suited our desired narrative. If you've ever been in that place where desperation feels like a cliff you're hanging by the nails from, you know something of what it's like to come to the end of yourself.

As stated earlier, Jesus experienced that moment while in Gethsemane.

The Lord, physically speaking, *did not* want to go to the cross. Who, with a sane mind, would?! While on prayerful knees in Gethsemane's garden, a distraught Son of God sought a "Plan B" from heaven. He had hoped for another way to save us. Just days before He would be crucified, things came to a head for the Lord. He had not only come to the end of His ministry, but seemingly to the end of His emotional and spiritual resources as well. If Matthew's account of Gethsemane reveals anything to us, it's the element of limitations Jesus felt in His *humanity*.

As a fully human person, Jesus was nearly undone by the enormity of what lay ahead of Him at Calvary. Yet even as His hope of averting the horror of crucifixion was denied, He never ceased to obey the will of His Father in heaven. There, within a garden, consumed by anguish, the Saviour uttered timeless words that echo in our hearts every time *we* choose the way of the cross and the way of its cost: "*... not as I will, but as you will*" (Matthew 26:39).

Every follower of Christ experiences moments when they must decide whether to obey the clear will of the Word of God or face the inherent cost of disobeying. Chances are, at some point in our spiritual lives we've had to trudge though our own personal Gethsemanes. God is always testing the mettle of our faith—the elasticity of our obedience and its pliability for accepting His will. It's not always easy to distinguish between doing what we are called to do and doing what we want to do. Our wants can distract us from what our true action should be.

We don't always want what God wants for us. One is never *born* a disciple; we can only *become* disciples. A mastery of self-denial is not something we develop while in the womb. None of us comes naturally equipped to embrace the kinds of sacrifice that our discipleship demands of us. Though we desire the good and godly product God wills to bring about in us, we often repel the processes He uses to implement it. Yet it is in those times when we've come to the end of ourselves that we reach the starting point of spiritual surrender and submission.

The will of the Father that brought Jesus great pain and heartache brought us the hope of forgiveness and deliverance from sin and eternal death. This would never have been possible if Gethsemane ended with an alternate storyline—with the Son of God deciding to no longer obey His Father at all times and at all costs. If heaven's gates remain open wide for redeemed sinners to enter through, it's because the Son of God resolved to have His arms *stretched* wide on the cross.

We never know what obeying God's will for us—even if our obedience requires that we suffer for Him—might mean to someone else who's observing that obedience. A younger believer may be emboldened in their faith and commitment to God by watching a more seasoned believer trust God through some painful and life-changing trial. For Christian believers throughout the ages, the indelible image of a bowed and broken Saviour in Gethsemane has meant literally everything to them. There we observe the greatest love we could ever know, embodied in the extent to which Jesus was willing to go to *demonstrate* that love. There we observe why the Lord is more than worthy of all honour, praise, and glory, and why He is worthy of our love *and* obedience. Certainly, the Lord thought *we* were worth choosing His Father's will over any alternative to the cross.

Identifying with Christ always means identifying with His sufferings and His call to take up *our* cross daily. Oswald Chambers wrote, "It is only though our relationship with Jesus Christ that we can understand what God is after in His dealings with us… God's way is always the way of suffering—the way of the 'long road home.'"[37]

In the Western world, it seems more difficult for us to accept suffering. We think it shouldn't exist. We rationalize that it is neither right, nor good, to experience pain. Such a mindset can adversely affect our faith as God's people. Yet even if our Christian experience comes to be defined by what it has cost us, God honours and blesses obedience along the way. We put ourselves in the best position to be honoured by God when we realize that obeying *His* will is always the best means to our end. And sometimes it takes coming to the end of *our* will and way (indeed, our very *selves*) for us to be able to obey God in difficult situations.

> CROSS-WALKING: Can you recall a time when you experienced your own *personal* Gethsemane? What was the outcome? How does the account of Jesus in the Garden of Gethsemane inform your love and appreciation for Him? Why does obeying the will of God sometimes cause us to suffer?

---

37 Oswald Chambers, "Partakers of His Suffering," *My Utmost for His Highest* (available online at https://utmost.org/partakers-of-his-suffering/; accessed 3/28/2021).

CHAPTER THIRTY-TWO
Simon's "Cross"

...they forced him to carry the cross.

—Mark 15:21

We're told in the Gospels that a man was chosen to carry the cross for Jesus Christ—his name was Simon the Cyrenian (from Cyrene, present day Libya). The city of Cyrene bears some biblical significance. In the book of Acts, Jews from Cyrene were present in Jerusalem when they heard the Lord's disciples speak in their native language at Pentecost (see Acts 2:11). Cyrene had a large community of settled Jews, who also had a synagogue in Jerusalem where they would go to attend feasts (see Acts 6:9).

One may wonder whether Simon's experience of having to carry the cross for a brutally beaten Jesus of Nazareth impacted him to the point where he became one of the "men from Cyrene" who later preached the Gospel to the Greeks, as documented in Acts 11:20.

Simon remains an intriguing and mysterious figure in biblical history.

Was he a Jew to begin with? Was he an African who converted to Judaism?

Did Simon's curiosity concerning Jesus' claims lead him to Jerusalem that fateful day?

Was he there to attend the Passover?

Was he an enemy of our Lord?

We don't know much, if anything, about this man. Yet his role in the drama that surrounded the last, agonizing hours of our Lord's earthly life before He was crucified is one that is unique as well as symbolic in the Christian spiritual life. In fact, Simon's act of carrying the cross for Jesus on the Lord's pain-filled path to Golgotha is memorialized in the fifth station of the Cross in the Roman Catholic tradition. Simon was not allowed to simply witness the suffering of our Lord. Rather, he will forever be known as one who was picked out of a crowd to relieve the Son of God of some of His suffering.

Perhaps some of us have wished that we could have been in Simon's shoes that day and be able to give something back to Jesus for what He had to endure for us. Simon couldn't have known how privileged he was to have the opportunity to touch and talk to the Saviour of the world—to have His precious blood stain his clothes.

By the time Jesus collapsed in front of Simon, His suffering had already reached many stages. If we were Simon (knowing now what we couldn't have known then), what would we have said to the Lord? Would we have immediately commenced preaching about who He really is? Would we have asked to be crucified along with Him? Indeed, as disciples, we *would* be—albeit in a spiritual sense (see Galatians 2:20). Or would we, in horror, have turned from the sight that Isaiah described as *"Like one from whom people hide their faces..."* (53:3)? How would we have handled the presence of the cross?

Jesus could have handled His cross in many different ways.

He could have got right to judging the authorities who abused Him, showering them with words that would have caused them to tremble and expire on the spot. With a piercing look, He could have slain those who jeered and wagged their blasphemous fingers at Him as He moaned and bled profusely. Jesus could have given them an ultra-convicting ten-point sermon on hell if He so chose to. Our Lord could have summoned all the angels in service to God to come down and relieve Him of His excruciating pain and the injustice of it all.

Yes, Jesus could have done a lot with the cross that fateful day—but what He *did* do, He did out of love for us.

We don't know what became of Simon from Cyrene. We don't know with certainty how the Cross of Christ touched his life, or what he did with what he saw (and carried).

The presence of the cross demanded that Simon *do* something. That fateful day, Simon had to carry it and walk the same suffering road as Christ. Simon may have been *forced* to carry Jesus' cross by the Roman officials, but we are asked to carry it by *faith* in the One who died on it for you and me.

Today the cross still demands that we do something, that we make a decision.

We can choose to trust the cross, or reject it; we cannot, however, afford to ignore it. Our individual destinies hang in the eternal balance. Jesus' sacrificial death for a sin-ridden humanity at Calvary demands a response from each and every person—the religious and irreligious alike. None of us desires to look upon suffering, let alone experience it. Nonetheless, Jesus bids that we come and die with Him; that we die to self (our old, fallen nature oriented toward sin) so that we may find our life (redemption) in the everlasting life we gain in Him (Matthew 16:25). When we do, we enter into the reality of what it means to take up our cross. To identify with the Saviour is to be willing to walk a similar, costly road of suffering that's characterized by our obedience to Him. Indeed, the way of the Christian spiritual life *is* the way of the cross. They are inseparable.

CROSS-WALKING: Why does the account of Simon from Cyrene having to carry Jesus' cross fascinate us still?

Have you ever speculated on why God chose this particular bystander? How was Simon's "cross walk" symbolic of ours in a spiritual sense?

CHAPTER THIRTY-THREE
"Hymn" 22

My God, I cry out… but you do not answer…

—Psalm 22:2

There's a popular saying within Christian circles that goes, "Trust in the dark what you learned in the light." In other words, the child of God must lean on their knowledge of His loving nature and proven faithfulness whenever the trials of life have them wondering where He is. The person who penned the Twenty-Second Psalm did exactly that. The context of the psalm lets us in on two duelling factors. First, the writer is surrounded by taunting and mocking meanies who are the furthest thing from choir boys; second, he is unable to perceive so much as a whiff of God's requested intervention. It's little wonder then why David's articulation in the psalm renders it a cathartic invocation for any disciple of Christ to pray during times of great testing.

David's frustration with the silence heaven was issuing him in response to his cries for help seemed to port his faith in a place where he began to think the unthinkable; he began to put on paper sentiments he'd once thought unspeakable. In his great season of danger and deprivation, David felt forsaken by his God. Although others may have deserved such treatment, he felt he did not. In his reasoning, David hadn't just struck a puddle of confusion—he had fallen into a veritable pool of incomprehension!

Lamenting the space he feels between himself and the Lord, David repeats the phrase, *"Do not be far from me"* (22:11, 19). David desired for the divine distance he felt deep within the core of his soul to be removed. With no signs of God's imminent rescue in sight, a white-knuckled David yet chose to cling to his knowledge of the Lord's faithfulness to His people in times past (22:3-4). David was able to turn from the temptation to interpret the *felt* absence of God as meaning that his God had *abandoned* him for good. No loving parent could leave their vulnerable child to fend for themselves—and neither, David believed, could *his* God!

In 1527, Martin Luther became ill with an elevated fever that left him with prolonged physical weakness, including chronic dizziness. The celebrated reformer succumbed to feelings of psychological abandonment as well as God-forsakenness. For Luther, the "Where is God?" inquiry would become an unwanted chink in his armour of faith. It was the prayers of family and friends that carried him through the spiritually dark season he found himself in. During this period, Luther composed the masterpiece "A Mighty Fortress Is Our God"—an enduring hymn that Christians worldwide continue to sing and proclaim with boldness and confidence.

As an ancient Hebrew hymn, what we have as Psalm 22 was a part of Israel's worship liturgy, where its collective stanzas were put to music. David, as he always seemed to, arrived at the same spiritual conclusion Martin Luther would centuries later. A psalm (or song) that begins with David emoting feelings of being "forsaken" ends with the glorious certainty that *"generations"* to come will acknowledge the *"righteousness"* of Almighty God (22:30-31). In one fell swoop of his pen, David goes from catering to despair to heralding the hope he ultimately possessed in the Lord's deliverance. How invariably uplifting this psalm must have been to the ancient Israelites when they assembled for corporate worship and religious observance!

As conveyed by its author, Psalm 22 reflects the plethora of seasons that compile the life and testimony of Jesus' disciple. Some of these seasons usher in spiritually-charged breakthroughs and victories, while others barrage our pilgrimage with unwanted instances that stretch our faith and trust in God. Accordingly, Psalm 22 provides an example of how the child of God can remain authentic before Him while entrenched in personal spiritual battles and turmoil. In his psalms, David often took to railing at God, using provocative words that are as honest as they are heartbreaking. So when we come up against deceptive thoughts—the kind that try to convince us that God has somehow checked-out in the middle of our plight—Psalm 22, like some of David's other writings in the Psalms, reminds us that we not only have a peer in David, but one in the Person of the Son of God as well.

The most authentic person to ever live, Jesus Christ, quoted the opening words of Psalm 22 while on the cross: *"My God, my God, why have you forsaken me?"* (Matthew 27:46).

The Twenty-Second Psalm prefigures the suffering of Christ at Calvary with all its situational as well as spiritual parallels. In addition to the gross forms of physical pain and agony the Lord endured while on the cross, He also experienced the silence of the Father and the void of any of His hands-on care. Like David, the Saviour of the world cried out to God, only to feel unheard and unassisted. And like David, our Lord also refused to believe that His Father had, in fact, abandoned Him. Instead, a dying Jesus entrusted both his finished ministry along with His spirit to the Father (Luke 23:46).

There's nothing more taxing to the soul than for it to be suppressed by tribulation only to sense that God is distant and has left us to our own spiritual devices. Yet there's ample evidence within Psalm 22—indeed the entirety of Scripture—assuring us that God will never leave us and most certainly will never forsake us, regardless of the situation. Near the end of the psalm, David shakes his fears and trades them in for a call to worship his worthy God. Despite his unsettling circumstances, it was clear in David's quieted heart that the Lord was trustworthy and remained the *"theme"* of his *"praise"* (22:22–25). May it be that whenever God moves *us* from feelings of despair to hopes of deliverance, such times will serve as opportunities for Him to put a new song in our mouths—a hymn of praise to our God (see Psalm 40:1–3)!

> CROSS-WALKING: Can you recall a time when, like David, you felt as though God had forgotten or even forsaken you? How does Psalm 22 aid us in practicing authenticity before God in prayer? How, in particular, was Jesus' suffering (just prior to and while He was on the cross) defined by David's words?

CHAPTER THIRTY-FOUR
A Stone Rolled Away

He has risen! He is not here.

—Mark 16:1–6

Following the Crucifixion, three women (the two Marys, along with Salome) approach the tomb where they know Jesus has been laid to anoint His body with spices for His burial. Upon their arrival at the place of Jesus' burial tomb, they ask an obvious question: *"Who will roll away the stone from the entrance of the tomb?"* (Mark 16:3). The fact that the women went with spices to anoint Jesus' body tells us they weren't expecting a resurrection to take place. It's also clear that they knew they didn't have what it took to muscle the sealing stone away from the tomb's entrance.

When we *spiritualize* the women's question as to "Who will roll away the stone...?," it translates, *How do we get to God?* Billy Graham would often say that it's the "most important" question we can ask in life. Sadly, it's one that many are giving little to no thought of as they race toward the grave.

There were those in biblical history who *did* make such an inquiry. After Peter preached the newly birthed Church's inaugural "sermon" (and a convicting one at that), many who were listening responded by asking the apostle, *"What shall we do [to be saved]"?* (Acts 2:37–41). The three thousand who came to faith in Jesus that day were cognizant of the fact that something was blocking their spiritual pathway to God.

If God is holy and we are human, how can we get from where we are to where He is? How can we prepare to go from this earth into eternity? In other words, *Who will roll away the stone prohibiting our entrance?*

The "stone" I refer to is analogous to the unbelief and indifference that cover and seal the hearts of those today who have yet to trust Jesus Christ for their salvation.

As mere humans and sinners, we are wholly incapable of removing the stone-like barrier of unbelief and rebellion that separates us from Almighty God. As in the post-Crucifixion Gospel accounts, this stone must be *supernaturally* moved!

The women arrived only to find the stone *already* rolled away with not a soul around—except, that is, for a certain angel who had now set up shop in the otherwise vacant tomb. There were not even any guards present. And where exactly, the women wondered, was Jesus? What would His body being missing mean for those who followed the Lord as His disciples? What may have appeared as a crime scene was really a *divine* scene!

Herein lie some of the main spiritual applications from the Gospel accounts of the Resurrection.

The women didn't need others to move the sealing stone away from the tomb's entrance. To state that another way: they didn't require *human* mediation to help them to get to Jesus. They didn't need to bring Him anything or do anything for Him. All they needed to do was *come* to Him. God, through the Resurrection of His Son, had already taken care of the rest!

So many people try hard to impress God and merit a good standing with Him. They feel that by doing so, the bad they've done in life will be balanced by any good they do. The hope is that the bar of God's standard will be lowered enough for them to get over it and get into heaven. It's a plan that, if it were not so hopelessly flawed from a theological standpoint, would make perfect sense.

In the days of the prophet Ezekiel, the Lord desired to restore his wayward people by giving them a new heart that would love and obey Him. The nation of Judah couldn't do enough to off-set the Lord's anger towards them for their idolatrous ways and unholy living. The Lord knew that the only way He could bring about the type of heart in His people that would please Him was if He did the spiritual surgery Himself.

> *... I will remove from you your heart of stone and give you a heart of flesh.*
>
> —Ezekiel 36:26

Today, the unbelieving still need a heart change, not a change in the number of times they'll do something "good" in the hopes of pleasing God. He wants all to come to Him, but we can only come to Him through faith in what His Son did for us on the cross. God doesn't require us to gain brownie points that cannot pardon or wipe out our sin and remove unbelief. Only He can turn a stone-hard unbelieving heart into a spiritually workable and surrendered one. Where hearts remain hard as rock and closed off like a sealed tomb to God's Redeemer, there can be no salvation. Jesus informed the Pharisees that by their refusal to believe in Him, they remained in their sin and without the hope of eternal life (John 9:41). Only Jesus could make a proclamation such as that—something He did numerous times in the Gospels.

Many acclaimed religious figures and spiritual leaders have come along over the millennia, but as popular as many of them were, after their deaths, they were never heard from again. Not so with Jesus. At His Incarnation, He was fully God but He had come in an entirely human body that was anatomically identical to ours. And even though the Lord was crucified, pronounced dead, and buried like any other person, He was gloriously resurrected and later ascended back into heaven.

The angel occupying the tomb as the women arrived to anoint the Lord greeted them with words Christians today greet one another with on Easter morning: *"You are looking for Jesus… He has risen! He is not here!"* (Mark 16:6).

God has not appointed those who believe in His Son to stay in their graves either (Psalm 16:10–11). We've been assigned to live on a much higher plane! This is what it means to live a resurrected life as a disciple of Christ. Therefore, we won't find Jesus in the place of death. No burial cave or coffin can contain the largeness and infinite Person of God. Some want to keep Jesus in the stable; others only remember Him as a figure dying on a cross, but those who know the Word of God and have put their faith in the Son of God know the real score: He is *risen!* The Bible says that in heaven, Jesus is interceding for us at the right hand of the Father, where He executes His divine power and authority. He is the *living* God. The stone that was rolled away now shows us *The Way*, to the Truth and Life that is in Jesus the Christ.

> CROSS-WALKING: Do you still marvel at the events surrounding the Resurrection of Jesus? How do you live out the power of the Resurrection in your life? How does knowing that God will raise your body to eternal life affect your perspective on death and dying?

AFTERWORD
Burning Hearts and the Emmaus Road

The final chapter of Luke features a moving story of two grieving disciples who suddenly found themselves in a rather deep, theological discussion with the Lord Himself—only they were kept from recognizing Him (see Luke 24:16). When Jesus inquired what His two disciples were discussing as they walked together, they began to rehash their version of the past days' events that had led to the Crucifixion of their Master, Jesus. Their hopes of Israel being rescued from the Romans perished with the otherworldly Nazarene on a cross. This fresh reality left these disciples despondent and devoid of both present answers *and* future hope. In addition, there was confusion surrounding what the women had seen—or better, had *not* seen, at Jesus' burial tomb.

Forgive me for adding to the Scriptures a little by imagining the kinds of heart-wrenching and equally head-shaking questions these two disciples were left with post-Crucifixion, even as a resurrected Jesus, with His identity veiled, walked beside them:

How could this Jesus of Nazareth die?

We were sure that He was God's man, that messiah had finally come!

He taught as no one else ever has—so authoritatively. He had all the answers.

> *What about all the miracles?*
> *All the demons He slew...*
> *How can this be? Why?*
> *What now? We even heard His burial tomb is empty! What does this mean?*
> *What is going on, God?*
> *What are we missing?*

After hearing enough of the forlorn disciples bandying around reasons why hopelessness should rule the day, Jesus responded with a hearty rebuttal.

> *How foolish you are, and how slow to believe all that the prophets have spoken! Did not the Messiah have to suffer these things and then enter his glory?*
> —Luke 24:25–26

The Lord went on to explain all the Old Testament accounts, from Moses to the prophets, that collectively draw a prophetic line of completion to the Person of the Christ. Jesus directed the two followers to the truth about Him that the Scriptures had already revealed. The point was that what had happened at Calvary was, in fact, *fulfilled* prophecy (see Isaiah 53:3–9). The disciples' dreams of their Master restoring Israel hadn't been derailed; they had become a reality, in the form of the Risen King of the Jews standing right in front of them!

The messianic hopes of God's people didn't expire at the Crucifixion of Jesus of Nazareth. Neither did our only hope for salvation get stuffed in a tomb along with the Saviour. Jesus Christ, God's answer for our sin and eternal spiritual death, *lives!* And because He lives, this life, as incredibly difficult as it can be, has been rendered endurable.

What the two disciples experienced as they walked the road leading to the town of Emmaus, characterizes the spiritual pilgrimage

Afterword: Burning Hearts and the Emmaus Road

of Jesus' disciple. The account underscores how we can look into the full scope of Scripture to discover and trace God's redemptive plans in history; even more, it shows us that when life appears to be tangled-up in uncertainty, the central figure in that redemptive plan, Jesus Christ, is still on the throne and in complete control of everything that concerns us.

Too often we sell God short. Our finite, rational concepts of God tend to contain Him. It's good to keep in mind that anything we say about Him could be as equally untrue as it could be biblically accurate. God is infinite and therefore not fully knowable. The full mystery of God cannot be captured in our thoughts and speech. (This was something the two disciples on the road to Emmaus discovered!)

Even if possessing a full knowledge of Him is not possible in this life, we can still know Him deeply. We must come to Him with open, submissive, and listening hearts. We must train ourselves to recognize when He is speaking into our lives. That is why Jesus wills to inject His presence into our difficulties, and appears to us on roads marked with dejection.

I once had a discussion with someone who struggled to believe that they were still a Christian. This person had made a profession of faith many years previously, but then years of problems and pain led them away from their faith. The person, now much older and very ill, began reading their Bible again. One night they had a vivid dream in which they were walking along a road with someone they identified as being Jesus. This person turned to Him and said, "I'm not sure I'm a Christian." In the dream, Jesus responded, "You must be; you're walking with me." It is in no way a coincidence that that dream has "burned" in the person I was speaking with ever since!

The two disciples recalled how they felt their "hearts burning within them" as they walked with Jesus on the Emmaus Road (Luke 24:32). The two wonder-struck followers of Christ came to realize that the unseen God was, in fact, present with them all along, fulfilling His promises. Author Brennan Manning calls this "living in the awareness of the risen Jesus," which enables us to "cope with the stress and sorrow of life."[38] Knowing what the Bible says about God's help when we experience times of trouble is one thing; trusting Him as He enters into these troubles and walks with us through them is quite the other.

As we travel our own Emmaus roads of dashed hopes and broken dreams, may we feel the Refiner's fire glowing within *us*. It's a burning reminder that God is eternal, ever-present, and unfailingly good for His unchanging Word—a reminder that there is no condition He cannot touch and no circumstance He cannot inform. On these roads, Christ walks beside us awaiting *our* invitation for Him to stay with us, break bread with us, interpret life for us, and give us hope. It's His presence on our Emmaus roads that turns our sadness into joy, and our mourning into dancing. Our "walk" of discipleship with Jesus, then, should never be confused with being just another religious "by the numbers" experience (i.e. do this, do that, as well as the other thing, and the pearly gates will open for you). The Christian spiritual life is not about doing "things" in order to get something or somewhere; it's about doing life with Jesus in anticipation of reigning with Him for eternity. It may not always be the easiest life to live, but it is the *best* life we could ever live—and the *only* one that leads to *eternal* life.

This is the *cross walk* we're called to as Jesus' disciples.

This is where the Kingdom of God and our window of time indeed collide!

---

[38] Brennan Manning, *Abba's Child: The Cry of the Heart for Intimate Belonging* (Colorado Springs, CO: NavPress Publishing Group, 2002), p. 89.

Also by Ron Mahler

A Sacred Rendezvous
ISBN: 978-1-4866-2051-7

Noise and trouble characterized the first century world Jesus incarnated into. Accordingly, He had a plan to combat the sirens of chaos blaring around Him: *solitude*.

As the twenty-first century tumbles more and more out of control, noise and trouble continue to define the times we live in. We require spiritual space where we can unplug from the currents of daily commotion. More than ever, we're in need of sanctuary and silence.

In *A Sacred Rendezvous*, Ron Mahler, with fresh and creative insight, takes you on a journey through the Gospels to revisit the pathways the Saviour used to escape to remote places in order to meet up with the Father. You will be challenged to go beyond merely observing that intimacy to realizing and craving it, personally and continually. From heaven's perspective, we'll likely wonder how we could've settled for anything less on earth than the most sacred of all rendezvous!

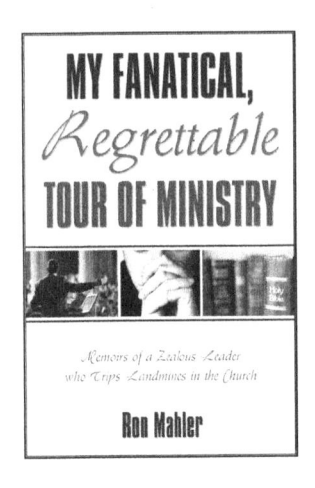

My Fanatical, Regrettable Tour of Ministry
ISBN: 978-1-77069-305-0

"Ron Mahler's sensitive heart and appropriate vulnerability are compelling. He is a pastor who has been through the battle and lived to tell about it. Good reminders for all of us who are striving to remain faithful as we march forward in a tour of duty for the Kingdom of God."

—Rev. Laird Crump

All Ron Mahler really aspired to be in life was an artist. The stars seemed to be aligned that way. However, after struggling to come to faith in Christ, God threw a heavenly curveball his way and issued him a swift call to the ministry. That's when his struggles really began. Not only were the first four churches he served in loaded with trials of many kinds, but he ended up leaving three of them *consecutively*, under duress. It was a long road back, each of the three ministries having had their own unique brand of disaster written all over them. Ron's greatest challenge went deeper than his need to forgive those who had hurt him; he also had to forgive himself.